Messages from the Other Side

Visit www.booksurge.com to order additional copies.

Messages from the Other Side

Joseph Tittel

2007

Messages from the Other Side

CONTENTS

ACKNOWLEDGMENTS

To my mother, Barbara Tittel, for not only being the greatest mother ever, but also for bringing me the validation I hoped for from the other side. May you live in harmony with the angels you so adored.

To my father, Bill Tittel, for encouraging me to move forward in my life. Thanks, Pop.

A special thanks to my partner Robert Breining for his support and for his faith in me and my work even when my faith waivered.

To all my family members and friends who have crossed over. Your messages from the other side have helped me to follow the path that my life is destined to be on.

To my spirit guides for being my best friends, for guiding me through my work, and most of all for having patience with me.

To Alison Kelley, for without her wonderful editing skills this book would not exist.

Finally, to the friends who began calling me "Spirit Man" and helping the name to stick. Donna(Momma Goose), Mike(Professor), Debbie, Mark, Bridget Murphy, Bill, Kelly, April, Mom D, Pam & Candice Breining for all the great help, Susan Duval,...I could keep going. Thank you, everyone.

To my Aunt Fran, for all the support, encouragement and mostly for believing in me. Thank you.

For My Mother Barbara

May you always watch over me like an Angel.

PREFACE

In this book I tell the story of my journey into becoming a psychic medium. I also give you a glimpse of my many experiences in communicating with the dead and in predicting future events. The experiences I wish to share are messages of hope and of healing—all of which I have learned on my path as a psychic medium.

The writings here are a kind of diary, chronicling my life experiences with the spirit world. My goal is to tell you, the reader, about my experiences in communicating with the loved ones of those for whom I have conducted readings as well as my own loved ones who have passed into spirit.

Everything I have written is an accurate portrayal of my experiences, with no embellishment or exaggerations. The people I have written about are real people, some of whose names have been changed for their requested privacy.

I hope this book opens your mind to the understanding that we go to another place after death and that our loved ones who have passed are still a part of our lives and see the things we have accomplished. I hope that sharing my experiences will help to give the healing and validation that you may need after losing a loved one.

CHAPTER I

How it began

I

How It Began

Visions

It began when I was about four years old. I saw a woman standing at the end of my bed in the middle of the night. She looked like an angel, but she had no wings. She appeared only on nights when I was sad or upset. Dressed in white, she had a bright loving light enshrouding her. I instantly felt warm and safe when she was in the room. She looked down at me in my bed and said "Don't be afraid, Joey, I'm here with you. You can go back to sleep." That's exactly what I did. I went back to sleep.

Looking back on this now, I might have thought that this lady was a dream. But I know she wasn't because I saw her again in the kitchen with my mother sitting at the kitchen table. I would say "hi" to her, and my mother would ask "who are you talking to?" No matter what my reply was, my mother would go back to her kitchen work. I continued seeing the apparitions until I was about seven or eight years old. Then the lady stopped appearing. I found out later exactly who she was.

One day, my mother was looking at some photos, and I remember pointing at one of the pictures and saying, "That's the lady who tucks me in at night." My mother didn't seem particularly curious about what I said. She simply replied: "That is your Grandmother, Mommy's mom. She is in Heaven now."

This woman wasn't the only one I saw over the years. There were others—a few were a little scary in that I didn't feel the warmth that I felt from the first woman.

Flying

I also had dreams that I was flying around my house both inside and outside. I thought nothing of these dreams until one particular night. During my dream I began floating above my bed looking down at myself lying there sleeping. I became a little confused but still I loved the idea of being able to fly. So I continued this journey of flight outside.

I began flying in circles around my home. What fun! Then I noticed something below that was not right. Earlier that day I had helped my dad take the trash to the curb. While flying, I saw the trash, but next to it was a chair with a box of trash on top of it. Everything else was in the exact place where we had put it except for that chair. I merely took note of this and went on my way enjoying my flying.

The next morning I ate breakfast, got my things together, and gave my mother a kiss goodbye before heading off to school. As I walked down the driveway, I took notice of the trash. Next to the trash that my dad and I had put out was a chair with a box of trash on top of it—exactly what I had seen while flying the night before.

Not until later in life did I find out that I was having an out-of-body experience—also known as astral projection. This is the ability of the soul to travel outside the body. All these things were a part of the preparation for my spiritual journey and introduction to the spirit world.

Premonitions

Not all of my experiences were of a spirit nature. I also had many psychic experiences, or premonitions. One stays in my mind more than any other. It was July 1977, and I was six years old. My parents had taken my brother, sister, and me to visit our aunt in Wildwood, New Jersey. She owned a small hotel across from the boardwalk. I still remember that week of fun in Wildwood, especially the water slide. On the last day of our vacation, my brother and I spent the whole day enjoying the thrill of the water slides—it was definitely my thing. After dozens of rides down, we were climbing the steps to ride down again. About halfway up the steps, I stopped and froze. Suddenly, I had an eerie and overwhelming feeling about the slide.

My brother grabbed at me and tugged my arm to hurry me back up the slide.

"What's wrong? Hurry up. Let's go!"

I panicked and said to him, "No. It's going to fall!"

He kept trying to persuade me to go back to the top, but I insisted that it was not safe and that the slide was going to fall. Eventually, I gave in and went back down the slide, but it was the last time I slid down that day.

The next day, my family and I packed up early in the morning and headed home after our great summer week. That night there was a big story on the local TV news. A water slide in Wildwood, New Jersey, collapsed and sent several people a hundred feet to the beach below. Fortunately, no one died, but several people were injured—a few severely. It was the same waterslide that my brother and I were playing on the day before—the same slide where I just knew something was going to happen.

Visions of earthquakes, storms, and many other tragedies would come to me throughout my childhood. However, some things I blocked out as being coincidences or as emanating from my own fears.

Recognizing My Psychic Gift

A question that is often asked of me is one of the most difficult to answer. "When did you realize you were psychic?" Or, "How long have you been psychic?"

I have always been psychic; I believe I was born with a gift. It has just taken me more than 20 years to identify it. The experiences I had as a child seemed nothing out of the ordinary to me. I didn't even come to realize what a psychic was until I was about 10 or 11—and only then after hearing my grandmother tell stories about it, which also made me question it.

Even though as a young child I tended to block out certain feelings and premonitions, the entire subject of the paranormal, psychics, and even communication with spirits completely fascinated me. I became even more intrigued when, at thirteen, I met a psychic at my aunt's psychic party. The psychic looked at me and told me that I was gifted and would eventually become a well-known psychic. I didn't believe her, but I took in the information. From that point on, I began working with a simple deck of Tarot cards. I read several books to help myself relate to the Tarot cards.

At first, it didn't work for me. I found it very difficult because there were so many cards. I had friends and family members shuffle the cards and I laid them out and read out of my book. I used this book for a few years before purchasing another deck of Tarot cards and giving it a shot without the book. The book seemed to complicate the interpretations. It seemed much easier to understand the cards without looking into the book every time I threw out a card. Without the book, I discovered an accuracy beyond belief! The definitions I was reading from the cards were not definitions you would find in any book. It all came naturally to me.

So, from about the age of 15 until about 19, I did readings for friends and family. At first people didn't want to take me seriously because I was so young. But this changed rather quickly, and friends were constantly nagging me to read the Tarot cards for them. Even the mother of my closest friend Bill would anxiously ask me to bring my cards over to read for her. At a young age, I had turned skeptics into believers. They insisted that the things that came up in the cards were completely accurate. At that time I figured it was just my ability to read the Tarot cards. I never thought of reading the cards as being a psychic and did not consider myself as such. I was about sixteen when I told my friend Bill's mother that her husband needed to stay off the roof and off ladders. I saw him falling and getting hurt. She warned her husband, but being a skeptic, he went up on the roof anyway. Unfortunately, he fell off the roof and was seriously hurt.

Still, I remained very skeptical of psychics. For some reason, I could not comprehend the whole subject of predicting the future or communicating with the dead. Nevertheless, the subject fascinated me. During my teen years, I ventured a little further into psychic exploration. Soon I abandoned my skepticism. I realized that psychics do exist and that there are people who can communicate with the dead. Being psychic was a gift that I had but would not come to understand until I was in mid-twenties.

By the time I was 19, my interest in metaphysics had grown to the point where my sister Tammie and I opened a small New Age shop. We sold incense, books, crystals, Tarot cards, and other esoteric articles. We decided to find a psychic to read out of a small room in the back of our shop. Her name was Deirdre and she was an amazing psychic. When we first met, she said to me "You should be doing what I do, and one day you shall." I heard that before! One day she insisted that I read Tarot cards for her. She was very impressed by the reading I gave and Deirdre repeated that I should be doing readings full time.

One day Deirdre called and said that she had decided that she was not going to come to work in our shop any longer. We urged her to stay, mostly because she was booked solid that day and many days following. Deidre said that I should take over and do readings for those who were scheduled to come to see her. I didn't know what to do and felt completely lost. "I can't do it," I kept telling myself. But then the first client walked in. This woman had no problem letting me read for her, especially since we were not going to charge her as much. She came out of the reading very satisfied and complimented me several times.

Subsequently, everyone who had come to the shop for readings that weekend was disappointed at first because they expected Deirdre. But after their Tarot reading with me, they seemed content and satisfied. That's when I began to read for others rather then just friends and family. Soon word got out and I became quite busy in the back of the shop reading Tarot cards.

Even then, I perceived myself as being basically a card reader, not a psychic. I read cards for about 6 years before I began to realize that I was definitely psychic and had something quite extraordinary. The feedback I heard from clients was excellent. I told them things that are not in any Tarot card book. I also began meditating and noticed I was getting information or psychic vibes without cards in front of me. The more I worked with my abilities and meditation, the more intuitive I grew.

I was about 25 before I finally realized that, yes, I am a psychic. The things that come to me are not as common as I had thought. I used the cards as a tool and thought that the information was coming from the cards. When I put the cards aside and read without them, I discovered I had no use for tools such as the Tarot. It would take years for me to discover the full gift that I was sent here with—the ability to communicate with those who have passed on and are now on the other side. Throughout this book you will see how I discovered that I had this gift.

Being a psychic has its advantages and its drawbacks. I keep hearing people say, "Shouldn't you have known that?" or "Didn't you know that was going to happen?" It doesn't work that way. Being a gifted psychic in my eyes means being here to use the gift to help others. It is not a gift to be used to help oneself or to reap benefits such as winning the lottery or picking a lucky horse. Still being psychic does have its benefits. Things come to me all the time—in thoughts and visions. These things help me in my daily life, just as they also help those who come to me for readings.

To this day, I find it hard to believe that I'm a psychic who basically talks to "ghosts." I don't actually call them ghosts, and they don't like to be called ghosts. What I do is communicate with spirits on the other side. The "other side" means heaven, the astral plane, or whatever you want to call it. It is sometimes difficult for me to try to interpret the information I receive and say these things to people because they often sound crazy to me. But to the people receiving the messages, it makes sense. I really don't know exactly how I do what I do. I just do it. I listen to my inner self, my soul, and my spirit guides.

We're All Psychic

We are all born psychic (where have you heard that before?) and spiritually in tune with the earth and all of its surroundings. But we are not taught to recognize this natural ability. Instead, we are taught to ignore it because we are just kids with big imaginations. Parents have forgotten that part of their childhood, so they no longer recognize the ability. I also believe and have experienced from myself and others that some of us are born with a "gift." These gifts differ in many ways. For example, some of us are born much more psychic than others. So it takes longer to block out this ability or to ignore it. The ability stays longer, so some people are fortunate enough to eventually recognize it. Still, many who are born psychically gifted end up blocking it out completely, not trusting it, or not using it consistently. If someone were to give you a gift of a new car, you would use it, wouldn't you? Like a gifted artist, or any other gifted person, you need to use your gift. I believe your gift is your destiny. I found out the hard way. My life was pretty much undecided and mixed up until I realized that my psychic gift is what I was meant to do in this lifetime. When I decided that was the path I needed to stay on, my life changed very much for the better.

You may wonder whether or not you or your child is gifted with psychic energy. I hope this book will enlighten you so you can decide for yourself whether you (or your child) are psychic. In this book, I want to share *my* experiences as a psychic medium and my communications with those who have passed. From this, I hope you will discover that your loved ones are around you and want to let you know that they are okay.

We all need to validate our own connections with our loved ones who have passed. We need to trust ourselves by knowing that it is not just our imagination. Most things come to us when we're not looking—like the gentle breeze infused with the fragrance of roses blowing past you as you do your chores in your home, for instance. Maybe it was your dearly missed grandmother's favorite scent. This can be a message from your grandmother's letting you know that she is okay and still around you every day.

Although many of my experiences have been intense, you need not expect this of your own experiences. Just know that each experience is special. Try to put behind you any emotions that you suffer because of a loved one's passing. Know that they are watching over you and wanting you to move on and enjoy the life you are still here to live. I hope that the experiences that I share in this book will help you to know that your loved ones are with you.

CHAPTER 2

Losing Mom

2

Losing Mom

My telephone rang Friday afternoon on October 8, 1999. It was my mother. The call wasn't unusual, but the conversation went into a very unusual mode. Mom was very big on watching soaps every weekday afternoon and would not tolerate interruptions, so I knew that this conversation would be short. But it turned out to be the longest conversation that she and I ever had.

Mom asked me about my weekend and whether I would have the opportunity to visit her. I lived an hour away and had to work the late bartending shift all weekend, so chances were that I couldn't make it. Then Mom told me with great excitement that today was the day she decided to quit smoking.

"I've been having problems breathing all week; it's starting to scare me. So I decided that I really want to see my grandchildren graduate, and I'm just fed up with the entire smoking thing."

Mom had slight emphysema, a good reason to stop smoking, although none of us knew this until later.

Mom and I continued talking for over an hour, long enough for her to miss her soaps. Very quickly, the conversation took a strange turn.

"Joey, I want you to know that I would like to be cremated and I want my ashes spread in upstate New York.

"What? What are you talking about?"

She went on, "I don't want a funeral either. I don't want anyone seeing me lie there dead, and no one needs to be crying over me. Besides, it's cheaper. Then she went on to tell me what possessions of hers she wanted us all to have, along with what she wanted her two grandchildren to have.

"Donate my clothes to Good Will; there are people out there who can use them."

I was jolted by the entire conversation. I said, "Mom, why are you telling me all this? You're not going anywhere."

Then she went on to explain.

"Out of my three children, I know that you will be the one who will carry out my wishes."

"Ok Mom, not a problem. I love you."

Then we talked about life and love and many other things. She told me how proud she was of me and how she knew that one day I would be very successful. It was a long and intense conversation. After a while Mom let me know that she was annoyed that I had to work all weekend. But I had no choice—it was Columbus Day weekend—the bar was going to be jammed. I had to work a double shift on Sunday, then another one on Monday. Mom didn't want to hear excuses. In fact, she hung up on me. She was pretty well known for hanging up when she was mad or did not have her way. I really thought nothing of it, and I started getting ready for work.

The weekend flew by, mostly because I was working long hours. New Hope, where I was a bartender, was teeming with people—tourists and locals. The weather was perfect, and the trees were beginning to change color. Monday morning I awoke and got myself ready for another long double shift. I had to open the outside bar at 11 am. Another busy day, for sure. And a busy day for my sister, too, who owned a metaphysical shop across the street from where I worked.

The Bad News

I felt great on this beautiful fall day. The music was playing at the bar, and I had my first customer. About an hour later, a friend of mine who worked in my sister's shop came in from across the street. Looking somber, he stood across the bar from me and said quietly,

"Your mom died."

"What!!?"

His words echoed through my head one more time, "your mom died."

I totally lost it. I walked up to my boss and told him, "I have to go, I have to leave!" I started to cry.

"Oh my God, what's wrong, you ok?" He said in his thick Italian accent.

"My mom died!" Then I ran across the street to my sister's shop, where she sat weeping in disbelief. My sister had gotten a call from my father, who told her about Mom.

I was very close to my mother, but my sister had many issues with my mother. We were both dealing with deep emotional grief in our own way. All I could think about was that my mother had hung up on me. I failed to reflect on the positive aspects of our last conversation. Instead, I beat myself up emotionally over the fact that I did not visit my mother and that she was angry at me about it. Mom left this world upset with the fact that I did not have time to come and see her. This was killing me. Again, I easily forgot how that last conversation was actually the best we ever had. My eyes fill with tears even now as I think about it.

This is what happened. My mom called 911 on Saturday because she had trouble breathing. When the ambulance arrived, the paramedics tended to her and suggested she go to the hospital. She must have felt a little better after getting some oxygen, which may be why she refused to go to the hospital. The next day, my mother called my pop to see if he would bring her something to eat. Although my parents had been divorced for 15 years, they remained great friends. Pop took her shopping, and they sometimes went out to eat. So Pop went to the local fast-food restaurant to get Mom's favorite bacon cheeseburger and fries, and then headed to her apartment.

But Pop arrived at an empty apartment. A neighbor came over and told him that she had been having trouble breathing and called 911. This time she actually took the paramedic's advice and went to the hospital. She left a note for my father, which I later found by her chair. Her normally beautiful handwriting was a scribbly scrawl. She had scribbled, "call to ambulance, going to hospital." So my father headed to the hospital. When he arrived, he was told that my mother had passed away. What an awful shock for Pop.

My mother had passed away from a pulmonary embolism—a blood clot in her leg that eventually moved to her lungs and blocked her breathing. Mom had neuropathy, which affected her legs and her walking. Therefore, she did not get around very well at her young age of 58. When they took her to the hospital, she got a shot for pain. Then she passed away with no one at her side. She had always said that she didn't want to die alone.

How could I not have known this? How could I fail to see it coming? I'm a psychic, I'm supposed to know these things. The amazingly long conversation on Friday should have told me something. I kept asking myself, Why? How come? How did I not know? Why was I not there for her? And a big one—could I have prevented this from happening? Such questions haunted me. Did Mom know that she was not going to be with us much longer? According to the things she said to me on Friday, she *did* know.

Soon after hearing about my mother's death, my sister, a few friends, and I went back to my house to continue our grieving. So many people in my house, but silence prevailed! Eventually, we told stories about my mother. We laughed and we cried. You could feel my mother's presence in the room. And she made it clear that she was there. Every time someone mentioned her name, the light above the dining room table flickered. If the light was on, it would go off. If the light was off, it would go on. This happened more then a dozen times in the few hours we were all together in my home. No doubt my mother was trying to let us know she was there.

Days, weeks, and months after my mother had passed away, the light continued to turn on and off by itself. I even went so far as to change the light switch to see if that had been the cause of the flickering. Then one morning I woke up thinking of my mother. When I went downstairs, I found the dining room light on. Maybe I had left it on last night before going to bed. At that exact moment, the light went off by itself. I knew for sure this was a sign from my mother. There is no convincing me otherwise. After that, the flickering stopped for good.

A Stern Message From Mom

A few months before my mother's passing, I received a ticket to see a famous psychic medium. A friend of mine told me all about this man and explained that he could talk to the spirits of those who have passed away. That really fascinated me. When she asked if I would like to join her for the show, I couldn't say no. The show was scheduled for early November. I remember telling my mother that I was going to see a psychic medium. The subject fascinated her, too. My sister was also interested and wanted to go along with us, but she couldn't get the day off from work. Time passed and I had forgotten about going to the show. I had forgotten about many of the things around me after my mother died. But my friend reminded and soon the time came to see the medium.

I was excited and hoped that I would receive a message of love from my mother on the other side. I became even more excited when at the last moment my friend couldn't go but my sister happened to be able to come—a sure sign that it was meant to be. I was confident that my mother would come through with a message. And with my sister there, too, it worked out perfectly. In my mind, Mom was definitely going to come through.

We walked into a large hotel conference room jam-packed with people. Lucky for us that we happened to get a seat up front about seven rows down and right along the isle, just perfect for the psychic medium to come up to us. The medium came in and started talking about himself and the work he does connecting with those who have passed away. All this time I was thinking about my mother and saying little prayers in my head to make sure she would come through for us. Suddenly a message came—loud and clear in my head.

"Joey"—Only my mother called me Joey—"Joey!!! You know more than anyone that I'm right here with you. There are people here who need this more than you. Shut up and listen, and know I love you and I'm here with you."

This message was clear as a bell. Yet, it was in my head and did not come from the psychic. I had no doubt that this was a direct message from my mother. To further corroborate it, every single person in the audience whom the medium went to with a message definitely needed it more than I did. A woman lost her son to murder. A man lost his wife when she fell down the stairs while pregnant. All the readings seemed to be directed in a very well-needed direction. It became apparent to me that the message from my mother was indeed a true one.

After the show I said to myself "I want to do what he does. I want to be able to help bring closure and validation to people who need it from their loved ones who have passed." Deep inside I knew it was the path I needed to be on. When the psychic medium stood and told his story of growing up and realizing his gift, it sounded like my story and experiences. Everything he was saying closely related to *my* life. This was when I began to think and understand the gift that I always had and never fully used.

CHAPTER 3

Messages From Mom

3

Messages From Mom

More than a year had come and gone since the passing of my mother. I was not doing much about readings at this point in my life. My focus was not on doing readings after some changes in my life led me to believe that it was not the path I was meant to be on. I soon found that thinking such a thing was a big mistake. It may not have been the path at that time, but one day soon I would find that it would be the path I was always destined to be on. Maybe I needed to get my own life together a bit first.

I was working in the restaurant business as a waiter and bartender, something I had been doing for several years. It took a good friend begging me to do a Tarot card reading for her before I finally gave in. Out came the Tarot cards and a whole lot of amazingly accurate information. Things came through like never before. This surprised me because I believed I had a "starting-over" fear. I was afraid I would not have the ability to do psychic work again. For me, this was a beginner's step in learning to trust myself and in having the confidence that I would be able to accomplish this goal. Why should I think that I would not be able to do something that I had once done so well? I should have known.

I Step into Mediumship

In no time at all I started getting more requests for readings. Customers from long ago suddenly began to turn up. Then, one day it just happened. In the middle of doing a reading for a woman named Barbara, I saw a beautifully dressed woman standing clearly behind her. Her lips weren't moving, but she began to tell me things. I described her in complete detail to Barbara, and the information just flowed through me. The vision was Barbara's mother, who had passed from terminal cancer. Information came through about birthdays, anniversaries, and the dates on which people had passed, along with names and lots of other information. Barbara was in tears, and I felt as if I had done something wrong. When she thanked me very sincerely, I realized that I helped her. I was able to validate things from her loved ones who have passed. This allowed her to realize that her loved ones are still with her, watching over her every day.

Every psychic reading I gave turned out to be nothing more than messages from the other side. I had my clients shuffle the Tarot cards, just as I had been doing for years. But now things had changed, and I felt that I was wasting time using the cards. There was no need. My psychic ability seemed to take over.

At first, doing readings for my clients was difficult because I had trouble saying some of the things that I saw and heard. I would think to myself, "These people are going to think I'm crazy." But when I just say what I see, it all falls into place. I may not understand what I'm telling my clients, but there is no need to understand. As long as it makes sense to them—which it usually does—that's what matters.

More and more people were coming to me for readings, and I was learning much from all these experiences. It became easier to interpret the messages I was receiving and to understand and explain them more clearly. This was an exciting time in my life. I really loved the fact that I was able to do this work and help so many people in the process. I decided that this work was what I wanted to focus on and the path I was ready to take. When I realized this as a goal, things at the local restaurant where I worked suddenly became tense. One day my boss had a few choice words for me; I turned and walked out the door never to return. This was not normal behavior for me to just walk out. I have bills to pay, responsibilities, and a life to live. For some reason, I didn't even think of the things as I was walking out the door.

A few days later, I was sitting at home looking through the want ads. I said a little prayer out loud,

"Spirit, I feel that the work I do now as a medium is the path I want to be on. If it is what I'm meant to do and the path I belong on, I am ready for it. Please, let it come."

Let me tell you, it came! The phone started ringing with people interested in my readings. From that day on, I went on my quest as a psychic medium, never to return to the restaurant business.

The readings became more intense; messages were amazing. At times, I finished a reading saying to myself, "God, did that really just happen?" Many of the spirits that came through were victims of murder or suicide with complete descriptions of what happened to them and who was responsible. Information came through from people who were supposed victims of suicide but who actually were murdered.

Often, people question me as to whether or not I am able to connect to my own loved ones. I can't just dial them up to chat on a boring day. They come to me; I do not conjure them up. When a client comes to me for a reading, I cannot necessarily connect with whomever they feel like chatting with, although I try. I tell everyone ahead of time, you never know who will come through and what message they will bring. It could be the son of a neighbor a few doors down. Sometimes they come through hoping that you will pass a message to someone else. Often they come through as a validation to let you know that I'm on the right track. So to answer the question, yes, I have received messages from my own loved ones, but no, I cannot talk when I want. It doesn't work that way.

I tell people over and over that our loved ones cannot just pop up in and say "Hello, I'm ok and heaven is wonderful." If it were possible, we would all be seeing our loved ones so often it would drive us mad. However, they are around us and often send messages—messages that we may choose to ignore or pass off as coincidence. Songs on the radio, lights that flicker or turn on and off, the phone, the television, and so many other things can be little signs that they are with us. If you don't look too hard, eventually the signs will be there in front of you. If you ask for a *small, simple* sign, you may just get it.

Mom Comes Through

What a hypocrite I was to stress this to people at a time when I personally expected a huge sign from my own mother. Aside from the fact that she did come through to me psychically with a message when I went to see the psychic with my sister, I expected more from her. Because of the work I am doing and how I've been able to help others, I felt I deserved to see her. I wanted her to pop in and say "hello," or to come in a dream, something big and significant. The more I dwelled on this, the longer I was missing the signs that were already there for me. But the day finally came when I received the biggest sign from my mother—one that I would never have expected.

Signs from Mom

It was a beautiful fall afternoon, my mother's favorite season. The trees were turning gorgeous oranges, yellows, and reds. It was a busy day for me, running errands and dealing with everyday stresses. I was on my way home after spending three hours washing my clothes at a laundromat. While I was driving, an overwhelming feeling of my mother's presence seemed to take over. I could have sworn she was sitting in the car next to me. I wished I really knew whether she was actually there with me in spirit or whether my mind was playing tricks on me. Then I thought about the fact that it was this time of year when my mother passed. Oddly enough I couldn't recall what today's date was so I reached for my cell phone to look at the date. The date stood boldly staring at me, October 10th, 2001.

"Wow." It just so happened to be the two-year anniversary of my mother's passing. At that moment I decided to give a long overdue speech right there in the car.

"Mom, if you're really sitting in this car with me right now, please show me a sign."

I rambled on some more.

"I realize now that I have been looking too hard and not seeing the signs around me. If you are really here, please show me a small sign to let me know that I'm not crazy and that you are indeed here with me now. If I turn on the radio and shuffle through the stations and just so happen to fall upon an Elvis tune, I'll know it is you. If I happen to see poinsettias along the road, I'll definitely know it's you—well, I guess it's a little early for poinsettias. Even if I see your birthday on a sign while driving home, I will know you are with me now."

By the time I got back home, I completely forgot about the whole incident. I went about my evening cooking dinner and watching a little television before going to my computer to check my e-mail. I booted up my computer, logged onto the Internet, and began downloading about twenty e-mails. I opened up my inbox folder and there it stood in bold writing at the top of my e-mail list—the Elvis Presley newsletter. I practically fell out of my chair. I no longer questioned whether my mother was riding with me in the car on the two-year anniversary day of her passing. Such a small simple sign as that had an intense impact on me in validating that my mother is with me from time to time. I realize that she cannot be with me all the time, as I would like her to be. I do have a brother, sister, niece, nephew, and father whom she would like to watch over as well. I do not believe that a particular loved one is around us in spirit all the time. These souls have other things to do, which are beautiful learning experiences.

When I felt my mother's presence around me in the car, I had asked her for a small sign to let me know she was around me. A small something that relates me to my mother and can simply be shown to me in odd ways, such as my e-mail. Who would have thought, honestly? To me that sign was so strong and Mom was definitely getting her point across. Whenever you happen to be focused on something such as driving and suddenly you have a thought or feeling of a loved one who has passed, talk to the person as if he or she were there at that moment. I find that any time that I happen to think of a loved one who has passed, he or she is indeed with me at that time. Ask for a few simple signs, don't look too hard, and it is guaranteed that one will come to you. Maybe this time you will recognize the sign and not choose to ignore it as so many of us do.

I talked about my experience with my mother coming to me in the car for a long time and still do. You would think by telling the story over and over again that I would at least get the date correct—especially since it was the date of my own mother's passing. For some reason I kept telling the story as happening on October 11 instead of October 10. Well, my mother was about to make sure I would never mix up the date again. She did something stamped with her own sense of humor. I can picture her laughing now. I try to explain to people that those who are in spirit don't have negative emotions. They couldn't be mad at us if they wanted to. I like to refer to it somewhat like Woodstock '69—love, peace, and happiness. And they do have a sense of humor. Don't be surprised if your missing keys were moved by your father who has passed.

More Signs From Mom

On the three-year anniversary of my mother's passing. I did several readings at a small party not too far from my home. This particular party took a lot of energy from me and stressed me out a bit. The ladies in the group were a very nice bunch, and we did a good bit of chatting. I told them the story about my message from my mother and mentioned that the anniversary of her passing was tomorrow. Now I realize I was wrong about that, which I found out when I got home

I drove home not at all thinking about the anniversary or the story that I told the young ladies that evening. I'm not one to dwell on the anniversary days on which any particular person has passed away. It is not something I think they want us to do. I know a lot of souls on the other side, and I don't know the date when any of them passed away. I only know my mother's anniversary because I think she implanted it in my head.

When I got home that evening, I kicked off my shoes, put my feet up, and began to relax. My roommate and I talked about the party and how everything went. I told him the story I told the girls about my mother being in the car with me and her anniversary. Then we went about doing our own things. He was sorting through a stack of his papers when a little card fell onto his lap. I heard him say "Oh my God." He had a spooked look on his face. He handed me the card and said "this is definitely a sign from your mother." It was the funeral card from my mother's memorial. On the back of the card was the date October 10, 1999.

That I was amazed would be an understatement. It so happened that it was October 10—a bold reminder from my mother that the 10th is the anniversary date of her passing, not the 11th. This could not have been a coincidence.

This incident of mine is another reminder that signs are here for us quite often, sometimes in front of us so boldly that we cannot miss them. Know that these types of things are true signs from your loved ones who have passed away. Know this deep in your heart and embrace it, for it is the truth. They are with us and want us to be aware of that fact.

My mother left me with two very nice signs, allowing me the closure and validation that I needed at the time. My mother's third sign would prove to be the most significant sign of all. It was a time of my life when there would be many drastic changes. In other words, it was a chaotic and depressing time in my life. If my mother were alive at that time, I would be able to turn to her for help and support.

Diane is a client who comes to me once every six months for a reading. We grew to become friends over the years. On this particular day, Diane came to my home for a personal reading. I remember that she looked around my living room and complimented me on all the Native American décor.

Diane said to me. " I have so much Indian stuff packed away, I should dig it up and give you some."

We went on chatting for a short time before I began Diane's reading. Her reading went very well and we chatted a little more before Diane went on her way. A few weeks passed, and it was time when my life was about to hit rock bottom.

When I came home one afternoon, I found a package sitting on my doorstep. It was from Diane. I had lots of things going on that day and I was in a rush, so I placed the package on my stairway inside and figured I would get to it later when I had more time. I thought to myself that it was probably some nice Native American piece. Something to add to my ever-growing collection. I had pretty much forgotten that the package was sitting at the bottom of the stairs until late one night.

I had had a really bad day and was pretty shaken up about many personal things. I couldn't get to sleep so I was lying around feeling sorry for myself. At one point, I began to think about my mother and how much I missed her. I was thinking about how nice it would be if I were able to call her up just to talk for a little while. Along with a really horrible day and a depressing evening, I had a feeling of emptiness and was missing my mother and wishing that she were there to comfort me.

Suddenly, I thought of the package Diane had sent me. Something was telling me to get the package and open it. I felt I needed to do this because it might cheer me up, and maybe I could get some sleep. So I crawled out of bed, went downstairs, grabbed the package, brought it back to my bedroom, and crawled back into bed. I procrastinated for a few minutes, then began to tear away the tape from the box.

When I finally opened the box, I couldn't believe my eyes. I began to shake and cry. The items in the box had nothing to do with Native Americans, as I previously thought. Better than that. The box had a book about Elvis Presley and was loaded with pictures and postcards from Graceland. Diane had visited Graceland and taken the pictures herself. I always wanted to take my mother to see Graceland because she was such a huge Elvis fan. Of course, I never had the opportunity to take her there. I was so stunned and could not believe that Diane had sent all these wonderful things to me.

It took me about twenty minutes to pull myself together. Then I came to realize that my mother in spirit came to comfort me. I knew that it was she had sent me to open the package. I also know that she most likely had much to do with the fact that the package sat unopened as long as it did. It was as if my mother knew that I really needed her comfort and a sign to show me that she was there. I found this to be one of the most extraordinary validations that I have ever received.

I wanted to pick up my phone on the spot and call Diane, to share this story with her and tell her how greatly her gifts helped me in a time of need. Too bad it was three o'clock in the morning! So I waited until later that same morning to call Diane, thank her, and tell her the news. She was just as amazed as I was. I wanted her to know how grateful I was to her and how much it really helped.

Signs Are There

There is no doubt that our loved ones in heaven know when we are in desperate need of their loving energy. You should have no question that there is some loved one with you in spirit during times of need. They try to comfort us with their energies when it will most benefit us. Still, they can only do so much where they are. Just because you don't get a sign or a validation as meaningful as the ones that I have described does not mean that your loved ones are not with you. Chances are that you have been looking too hard, or maybe not at all. Remember things that your loved one enjoyed. For instance, my mother enjoyed Elvis. Remember the smell of their perfume, the sound of their laugh. Know that when you happen upon the things that they enjoyed or you walk through the familiar scent of their perfume, they are reaching out to you. They are letting you know in the simplest way that they are with you when you need them to be.

The experiences I've mentioned about messages from my mother are only the ones that had a great impact on me. Many more experiences have made me feel the presence of my mother around me. There were times when I thought of her and a light would flicker, or I would *sense* her around me. At times, I would hear a song on the radio that connected me to her. I have learned to "see" and not have to "look for." I have learned to just know when my mother is around me. I found this to be true for other loved ones I have on the other side. I've come to know when they are with me at a particular moment in my daily life. I even let them know by talking to them. Try it. It's fun.

Even though my mother is no longer with me in the physical world, she manages to teach me new and exciting things. She has taken me to places and levels I never thought I would go. In order to learn in school, you need to pay attention. So pay attention to your surroundings and your spirit and see how much more you can learn. Knowing this really has a positive impact on my daily life. If you have not yet learned this, maybe my writing about my experiences will help you with yours.

CHAPTER 4

Connecting With Family

4

Connecting With Family

My Aunt Fran and I are very close and have been since I was a little child. She played a huge part in helping me realize that I have a psychic gift. To this day she calls me when she has questions, even when she loses something. I just happen to always be able to find whatever it is she has lost. I have to thank her for her continued support and faith in me as a psychic medium.

From Skeptic to Card Reader

As I mentioned in chapter 1, when I was about 13, Aunt Fran had a psychic reader come to her home. Her name was Gail, and she was very well known in the South Jersey area. She had even been known to do readings for Cher when she came to Atlantic City to do a show. At the time, everything Gail told me seemed to make no sense at all. She told about many things that would come to pass over the next 15 years, but one thing she said really stuck in my mind. Gail turned to me, looked right into my eyes, and said,

"You have a very special gift. One day you will become a professional psychic."

Hah! You kook, I thought to myself. I was a complete skeptic. I went to see the psychic out of complete fascination for the unknown. I really didn't give a thought to anything she said about my future. It just didn't make sense to me. One thing she said jolted me, however. She told me that I had just purchased a deck of Tarot cards. With that, she was right on target. She went on to say that they were not the right cards for me, that soon I would find the right ones and would eventually not need them anyway. As time would tell, she couldn't have been more accurate.

I have to chuckle when people tell me they are skeptical about psychic abilities and connecting with those who have passed on. I was, too. Who wouldn't be? Sometimes it's all a little hard to believe. Unfortunately, there are some bad and just plain fake psychics. We shouldn't let these bad apples make us nonbelievers. There are many true and gifted psychics. I'm not saying *not* to be a little skeptical, but at least open your mind to all of this.

Only a few years after my reading with Gail, I started to read Tarot cards quite frequently. At about age sixteen, I was told to tell my Aunt Fran a few things in a card reading that were going to come to pass very shortly. I told her that she and my uncle would soon be building a new home from the ground up. Within a few weeks, lightning struck their home, and it had burned to the ground. Within months Aunt Fran and Uncle Harry began building their new home from the ground up.

Over the years I told many friends and family members of events that would soon come to pass in their lives. However, I prefer not to do reading for close friends and family members. Often, they don't want to listen, or they simply disregard any information they don't want to hear. Nevertheless, they all still call and ask me questions when it comes to an important issue in their life.

Uncle Harry

My Uncle Harry was a fun, happy-go-lucky guy. Everyone liked him. He would come to all the family parties and even came to visit me at the bar where I worked. All the regulars in the bar called him Uncle Harry. He could make anyone laugh. Even at my mother's funeral service, he brought laughter to a very depressing atmosphere. But Harry really liked to drink. Eventually, the drinking led to his death.

Uncle Harry was given less than a year to live because of severe liver problems. His health worsened day by day. He ended up sick in bed for a long time. Even though I truly believe that when our time is up and God is ready for us, we pass on to the other side, I also believe that some people fight death to stay close to the ones they love. Some people are just not ready to go, and they seem to deny God's will. Uncle Harry was one of those people. He lived at least three times longer than the doctors had predicted. They were amazed that he was able to hold on for years.

For months before his death, Uncle Harry talked about death with Aunt Fran and about the angels coming for him. He talked about angels being in his room. My aunt had a very hard time with his being sick. She didn't want to let him go.

Saying Goodbye

Aunt Fran came to realize she was holding on to Harry. One day, while Harry was drifting in and out of consciousness, she went into the bedroom and told him that she knew it was time and that she understood she was holding on to him and didn't want to let go. She then gave him permission to move on and be happy. She told him to go to the place where there is no more pain, no anger, no hate, and no negative energy, a place where nothing but love and happiness dwells, a place of beauty and tranquility. Then my aunt went outside as she did each week when the landscapers came to cut the lawn to tell them to keep it down around Harry's window, that Harry was sick and sleeping. However, this time she said it differently.

"Could you please keep it down? Harry is dying."

When Aunt Fran returned to Uncle Harry's room, she discovered that he had finally crossed over. This is how I learned that sometimes the dying hold on because *we* are holding them here. Sometimes we are the ones who have to let go. You can say your goodbyes and know that the person will remain a part of you, your heart, and your energy. Tell them to go, and allow them to do so. Tell them about the beauty in the light and to go to that light. Give them the permission they may need, and someday someone will do the same for you.

It isn't forever; they wait for us on the other side. So, even though you really love someone and don't want to let the person go, think about whether you yourself would want to be a terminally ill person just hanging on.

This is also true when it comes to pets. During my readings, pets are very often mentioned and want to be acknowledged as being on the other side with our loved ones. Sometimes they come through with their very names or appear to me so I can describe them to my clients. Of course, many pets were put to sleep, and many people have personal issues about putting their pet to sleep. From my experience with this, these pets and other souls in heaven do not want us to have this issue. You helped them along; you took the pain away from them. This is not held against you in any way.

Some people have made the difficult decision to take a loved one off life support. This should not cause guilt or pain. The person was helped to move on. If God did not want that person or if wasn't his or her time, then the person would stay and not be taken from us. When our purpose is fulfilled—whether we are three or sixty-three—God will take us to the other side. We should actually be happy about those who have crossed over and need not think they would be mad or upset with us. They do not hold these types of negative emotions in heaven.

Surprises

One of the drawbacks of the work I do is that I don't always remember the things I say to people. When I do a reading, the information flows through me without much of a thought process. Therefore, the only things I remember are things that astound me. Things that have me saying to myself, "Wow, that really happened?"

Aunt Fran and I talk almost every day. We were having a typical conversation one day when, Boom! There was no doubt that Uncle Harry was there.

I felt Uncle Harry's presence very strongly, and then words just started coming out of my mouth. What could I possibly say to her from him to allow her the validation that it truly was Uncle Harry? Through me, he mentioned to her the last thing she said outside the window to the landscapers that afternoon when he passed away.

"Could you please keep the noise down, Harry is dying."

Only Fran knew this, no one else—not even me. This was a very important validation for my aunt.

This was not the only occasion that Aunt Fran had a validation message from Uncle Harry. On October 14th, a few years after my uncle had passed. I was home doing some cleaning around the house when Uncle Harry came to my mind. All day I felt sort of hounded by thoughts of him. I even called Aunt Fran to see why he was around. No luck. She wasn't home. I tried several times and then left a message. Eventually, she returned my call. I told her,

"I think Uncle Harry is around today and wanted me to call you for some reason."

She said, "Well today is his birthday, you know."

I have to admit that I didn't know. I'm horrible when it come to dates, especially birthdays. So I told my aunt that this was his way of letting her know he is around today and all the time. If you knew Uncle Harry, you would know I would be the one he would come to taunt and have fun with in order to pass messages to my aunt.

Crazy Talk?

When I'm doing a reading, I often tell my clients that the crazier something sounds to me, the more I know it fits. Here is an example.

I was in Philadelphia doing a reading for a group of about 10 women. Most were not related to each other. I remember my focus came to be on two women sitting next to each other in the back of the room. I was connecting with their brother who had passed. He kept showing me the Fonz from "Happy Days," with his thumbs up saying "Hey!" I really had a hard time saying this. I was thinking to myself "these women will think I'm nuts." Well, I said it anyway.

Everyone looked at me as if I were crazy, just as I thought. Then out of nowhere, the two women in the back burst out laughing, and crying, too. "Please elaborate on this for us," I asked. They explained that their brother had had a nickname. Every time he walked into a room he would stick up his thumbs and say "Hey!" So they called him "the Fonz."

One of the major problems I had in understanding and using my gift as a medium was learning to just say what I saw or heard. No matter how crazy it sounds, I need to just relay the message. If people don't get it right away, they'll get it later. Every message is an important message no matter how big or how small it seems. Sometimes it may be only a birthday or the date of a passing. But the underlying message is to let the person know that there is another side, another place, possibly called heaven—and that our loved ones are around us, watching over us.

Passing It On

I find that many messages that come through in readings are messages that are to be passed on. There have even been times when the person for whom I was doing a reading received nothing but messages for someone else, such as a friend or other family member. They have their reasons on the other side for what needs to be passed on. I don't know their reasons, but I'm sure they're important. If they want someone to be there, they will insist on that also. I have gone to do family group readings in which a sister or mother didn't come for the reading. Their loved ones in spirit in turn forced me to call the missing person on the phone and make them a part of the reading.

Even though I tell people they should not feel obligated to pass a message on to someone still living, I'm sure spirit would appreciate the gesture. A client of mine recently told me about a message I gave her with the insistence that she pass it on. She told me she couldn't do it. Her friend came through who passed rather young from breast cancer. All the details came through in the reading, including the name of the woman's husband, who is still living. One message was that she wanted her husband to know she made it to the other side. My client insisted that there was no way she could pass on this message because her friend died so many years ago. She didn't even know where her friend's husband lives. The woman in spirit came through thanking her for passing the message and saying that she will have the opportunity to do so. The reading ended and the woman went on her way.

A few months had passed and the woman came back to me to share her story. She explained that there really had been no way for her to pass that message, and even if she could, she would feel out of place. One day she decided to go to the cemetery to leave some flowers for her friend. When she walked toward her friend's plot, she noticed a man standing there. It was her friend's husband, whom she hadn't seen since her friend passed. She told me she got tongue-tied and really did not know what to do or say. Then her courage seemed to come out of nowhere, as if her friend were actually there in spirit.

She began a friendly conversation with the woman's husband. Then she mentioned that she went to a psychic medium and his wife came through. She said he reacted kind of weird, as if he were offended. He said, " I don't believe in that sort of thing." Then she asked him,

"Can I at least just give you the message that your wife gave to me for you and you can do with it whatever you like?"

He agreed and she told him the message.

"She said she is fine and made it to heaven and she watches over you and the children."

He seemed a little shaken up and then went on his way. She told me that the expression on his face showed that the message hit home real well. Chances are that, like many people, the man began to lose faith in there being a heaven or even a God. Many who have lost loved ones come to believe that if there is a God, why would he take my wife/husband away from my children and me at such a young age? This is quite understandable given certain situations.

We need to have faith and come to understand that God has other work for our loved one, whose mission here is finished. The woman in spirit wanted her husband to understand that she is in heaven and that it *does* exist. Hopefully, he will be able to move on with the faith that she is still with him, watching over him and the children, and that one day they will see each other again.

CHAPTER 5

Finding Heaven

5

Finding Heaven

Heaven or, as I refer to it, "the other side," happens to be a beautiful place—a place where negative energies do not exist as they do on earth. People who have had near-death experiences and claim to have seen the other side all describe similar experiences: the white light, the angels, the colors, and all the beauty. This is great assurance for us that life on earth is not the end. There is an afterlife, and it is a place where we all meet up once again.

In my young adolescent years, I found this just too hard to believe. Death and dying were a big fear deep inside of me. Question after question came to my mind as to whether there actually *is* an afterlife or a place called heaven. The thought of death simply made me shiver with fear. Again and again, thoughts of death and the possibility that there is no life after death would intrude into my mind. Then after only a short time passed, my thoughts shifted toward a direction of belief. The experiences of seeing spirits and feeling their presence had a lot to do with it, along with a very intense experience that would allow me the privilege of saying, "I saw the other side."

At age 22, I was running my own New Age shop in my home town of Levittown, Pennsylvania, which was situated on the corner of a run-down shopping center. Here, two new friends, Paul and Sharon, entered my life. One sunny afternoon, Paul came into my shop and we started talking. Later that day, he came back with his girlfriend Sharon, and the three of us got into another discussion. It turned out that they were friends of Vince, an old friend of mine from high school, whom I hadn't seen in years.

Finding Vince

One day, Paul, Sharon, and I were hanging out together driving somewhere in Paul's car. I don't know where we were going. We happened to make a turn onto Vince's street, and he happened to be standing outside his house with a few friends. He waved us down; we pulled over and chatted a bit. Vince and I had not seen each other since high school. We were great friends and were known for getting into trouble together in class. We hung around together a lot throughout high school but lost touch after graduation, as often happens. After we all had a nice conversation, Paul, Sharon, and I drove away. That was the last time I saw Vince alive.

Nothing seemed to be wrong with Vince at the time we met on that sunny afternoon. He looked good; he smiled and laughed. Everything seemed fine with him, and maybe it was. Within just a few weeks, things must have gone terribly wrong for Vince. A certain gloomy October day was about to become even gloomier. On that day I received news from Paul that Vince had taken his life.

Apparently, Vince was having a hard time with his girlfriend, to whom I believe he was engaged at the time. Maybe she broke it off. There was certainly a lot more to this story, but it would remain a mystery to most of us. There were no signs that Vince was upset or depressed. He said goodnight to his sister and mom and went to his bedroom. That was the last time they saw Vince alive. When Vince got to his room, he opened a bottle of liquor and began drinking heavily.

From that point on, we know very little about what happened. Vince grabbed a gun, either a rifle or a shotgun. He climbed out his bedroom window and headed to the woods at the bottom of his street. There he found a spot next to the creek to sit up against a tree and contemplate whether or not he should take his life. At some point, his finger pulled the trigger, and the sound echoed through the neighborhood. People heard it, looked out their windows, and went back to their television sets. The next morning, a neighbor walking his dog came across Vince's body. Soon after, I heard the terrible news. Vince's entire family was horribly distraught over Vince's death. The circumstances of his death made it that much harder. His poor mother. They were very close, and he was the only son. So, what was to happen to Vince's soul? Was he doomed to hell as many would think? Definitely not, from my belief and experiences.

I believe in my heart that everything is meant to be—no matter how horrible. I can't explain why. One day, when we cross over to the other side, we'll learn the answer. Moreover, I don't believe that those who die by their own hand go to another place that reaps horror—like the so-called place of hell—whether or not it really exists. I believe these souls go to the same place that we all go.

Heaven and Hell...or Not

Whether or not there is a dark place where so-called "bad" souls go is not clear in my mind. People often ask me whether I have ever connected to this place called hell in a reading. The answer is no, and I hope I never do. I believe there *is* a darker place, the "lower plane," as I call it. What exactly decides the destiny of the souls that are sent to that level is beyond my knowledge.

One can think of the other side as being set up like a school—preschool to twelfth grade. I believe that we are all here to learn a lesson, probably many lessons. When we have finished learning, our time here is up. Even if we fail to learn our lesson, we eventually move on to the other side. If we pass—that is, if we learn our lessons—we move to the next higher grade.

When you progress through all grades and master all lessons, you graduate and move on to higher education. This means not having to come back to earth again. What happens when you do not learn the lessons you were meant to learn? You fail. You go back to the same level, or maybe a lower level, and you come back and try again until you get it right and learn the lessons that you came here to learn. A person who takes his or her life probably did not learn these life lessons and may go back several levels as a sort of punishment . But the opposite could be true. No one knows.

My own experience in communicating with souls who have taken their own life is that they regret it. It is possible for a soul who has died by suicide to get stuck here on earth and not be able to go into the Light. This could have been what happened to my friend Vince.

Sending Vince to the Light

About a week after Vince had taken his life, some very interesting things happened. Meanwhile, a big party was held to raise money for Vince's family to help with the funeral and gravestone. The party went well; there were both tears and happiness. It helped the family with their healing process. This is where first I met Vince's sisters and mother. During the next few weeks, I was to become close to Vince's mother. From this closeness, many things came to the surface.

Vince's mother asked me question after question seeking to know whether her son's spirit crossed over. Through meditation, I found that the answer was a big "no." His spirit was basically distraught and confused and had not crossed over to the other side. Coming from a strict religious background and belief system, Vince's mother was in despair about whether he would make it to the other side.

What really happens to our souls at the exact time of passing? What we learn from the accounts of people who have had near-death experiences is that we see the Light. Not all souls choose to go into the Light. This is how I would define the difference between a spirit and a ghost. A spirit is one who crosses over to the other side. A ghost is one who is either stuck here or chose not to cross over. Why do some souls *not* want to cross over? There are many possible reasons. From my experience, ghosts are usually spirits that have been killed tragically or did not move on because they were holding on to someone on earth—maybe a loved one. The Light may be there for just a short period of time. For the Light to re-appear to these lost souls, we must pray and try to get them to cross over to the other side through the Light.

My friend Vince pretty much refused to cross over at first. His soul was completely ravished from the experience. He was pretty intoxicated at the time of pulling the trigger—so intoxicated that maybe he didn't mean to pull it at all. When his soul left his body, he realized what he had done and the effect it would have on his family. This is when the spirit begins to become distraught, and a sense of being lost takes over. The spirit does not know what to do or how to fix the mistake. The spirit wanders around, replaying the event over and over. This is what happened with Vince.

When I realized that Vince did not cross over and that his spirit could not rest, I felt the need to do something. How could I help him? There had to be something I could do. Talking to Vince's distraught mother gave me an extra impetus to find a way. So with some meditation and help from my spirit guides, a plan came through. A white candle, some special oils, incense, and some good prayers were the tools I would need.

On a calm October evening, I drove alone to the cemetery where Vince is buried. Sitting on the ground, I faced the headstone directly. I had some incense burning and I had the white candle in one hand and the oil in the other. Eyes closed in meditation, I began to pray, rubbing the oil all over the candle.

Please, Lord, bless this candle with your Light.

As it burns, allow the Light to shine brightly.

May it help Vince to cross over into your hands.

Please, Lord, bless this candle with your Light.

Then I placed the candle in front of his headstone next to the incense. I closed my eyes again and meditated a little, trying to picture the Light in my mind and Vince heading toward it. I opened my eyes, lit the candle, and began to pray again.

Please, Lord, hear my prayer.

As this candle burns, may the light above shine brightly.

May it help Vince to cross over to the other side

Into your hands, good Lord.

Then I sprinkled a little oil in a circle around me and prayed some more.

Please, Vince, if you are here with me now, hear my prayer.

I know and feel that you can hear me.

Please move on to the other side.

Go to the Light, Vince.

There are loved ones waiting for you there.

Your family will make it through this.

They want you to cross over and be safe with God.

Please, Vince, please go to the Light.

I sat a little longer meditating and thinking and hoping for Vince's mother's sake that this would help him cross over. I did have a sensation of a presence during my prayers, but I wasn't sure whether it was Vince or someone else. After all, I was in a cemetery! A half-hour later, I decided my work was complete. I left the white candle at the gravesite to burn for seven days. It was a special prayer candle that came in a tall glass and supposedly has the ability to burn for seven days straight.

The next day, I received a phone call from Vince's mother. She was frantic.

"Joseph, I'm extremely worried. You put the white candle on Vince's grave, right?"

"Yes."

"Well, the candle keeps going out. I keep trying to light it, but it keeps going out."

"It's been very windy today." I was a big help!

"What can we do? Is this going to hurt what you have done? How can we keep it lit?

The phone call caught me off-guard. My mind went blank. Then, Vince's mother suggested using an eternal candle, which you buy for cemeteries. A little too expensive, I said. I thought about it for a few more minutes before coming up with a solution:

"How about if I go back to the cemetery. I'll get the candle, and take it home with me. I'll do another prayer and keep the candle lit at my house. This way it will stay lit, and I can keep an eye on it. It will be fine that way. I already did what I needed to do at the cemetery.

After convincing her that this would work, Vince's mother thanked me and ended the conversation. After work that day, I went back to the cemetery to retrieve the candle from Vince's grave. There it sat, blown out and cold from the wind. I picked it up, still a little slippery from the oil, said hello to Vince, and drove home. On my way home, I really felt as if Vince was in the car with me. It was a strong feeling, a depressing type of feeling.

At home, I anointed the candle with oil once again. Then I lit some incense, repeated my prayer, and re-lit the candle. At least I tried to re-light it. The wick was damp from the cool October wind. Over and over I attempted to light the candle; eventually, I got it lit. Still feeling the presence of Vince around me, I placed the candle on my bedroom dresser, where it was to burn without interruption for at least the next six days.

After five days, the candle was still sitting on my dresser flickering through the night and day with no interruptions. Vince's mother called me once again to say hello and also to thank me for everything that I had done. I assured her that the candle and prayers seemed to be working and that his energy was still present, but was definitely calmer. Since his energy was still present, it was more than likely that Vince did not cross over to the other side. But there was still another day, and we would continue our prayers that evening hoping for the best outcome. Then his mother went on to explain to me her recent experience with her son.

"I always bought Vince new lighters because I don't like the smell of matches. He was the only smoker in the house. The other night I was home alone in my bedroom when this smell overwhelmed me. It was the smell of burnt sulfur from a match. I knew there was no one in the house, but I got up and went to the kitchen to look. The kitchen is where Vince always went to smoke, or he would go outside.

As I walked into the kitchen, the smell of sulfur was even stronger—as if someone had just lit a match. I happened to look down on the kitchen floor, and you wouldn't believe what was lying there. A pack of matches! Lying right next to the pack was a single match that had been lit. I really believe that this was Vince trying to tell me something."

I said, "He is just desperately trying to let you know that he is around you, probably trying to apologize for what he had done. This may sound a little crazy, but he may be waiting for you to forgive him so that he can cross over."

She agreed with me and assured me that he does indeed have her forgiveness. Once again I informed her that she should continue her prayers, and I would do the same.

Eight days had passed since the beginning of my prayer and candle lighting at Vince's gravesite. When I returned from work, something really puzzled me. I found that the candle I had lit for Vince was still burning brightly, and the flame was flickering vigorously. From my experience with these candles, they don't burn that long. You're lucky if you can get the full seven days. They usually end up burning for only six days. Even with the candle going out repeatedly at the cemetery, it would not normally have lasted several extra days.

That evening before going to bed, another prayer for Vince set me off into a deep sleep. The next morning I found that the candle was still strongly flickering, radiating a bright light. Why would this be? How could this be? I never heard of such a thing. And it continued. Two more days would pass before the candle eventually burned out—on the evening of the eleventh night. What kind of sign was this? Did the candle and the prayers work? Did my friend Vince finally cross over to the other side? I think so. But only the Lord knows whether Vince actually did cross over to the other side.

The energy was calm now, as if Vince actually made it to the other side. I visited his grave once again, and this time it felt nothing like before. There was no presence of sadness and chaos as at other times. In addition, I did not sense Vince's energy with me. Did Vince cross over to the other side? Soon my questions would be answered, and I would receive the most significant validation I would ever have or need as far as my beliefs in the existence of an afterlife.

Validation Visit

It was a normal evening like any other when I went to bed. But something amazing took place in the middle of the night while I was asleep—a dream like never before. In the dream, I was in complete darkness, as if there was no existence other than my own. Then I seemed to be floating toward a destination. Suddenly a light appeared at a distance. It appeared to be coming closer, but actually I was floating closer to the light. Clouds of beautiful color took on formations around me as the light became brighter and more intense. Although the light was very intense and warm with a loving peaceful energy, it did not hurt my eyes. Then slowly I came to a stop and gazed at the beauty that surrounded me. Wow.

Off in the distance toward a much brighter light, I saw the shadow of a young man. Slowly, the shadow began to float toward me from the much brighter light. A sense of love, joy, happiness, and every good feeling a person can possibly feel overwhelmed me. It felt as if angels were singing all around me with voices such that I had never heard before. Then, the shadow of the young man became much clearer. It was Vince. He floated right up to me and greeted me. I heard everything he was saying, but his mouth never moved. I felt angels around me, but didn't see anything but Vince, the bright light, and beautiful colors. I felt the voices of the angels singing, but didn't hear them. Then Vince went on to say to me,

"I want to thank you for your help and for helping my mother. I'm ok now. I'm here and I'm safe and I'm happy. Please let my mother know this if you can. Thank you again for everything."

Then he gave me a hug, a hug that felt as if I was touched by an angel—something that I never felt. As he pulled away, tears were running down both our faces. Even the tears were like nothing I had ever experienced. Then Vince turned and floated back toward the bright light. A man and a woman took his hand, and the three disappeared into the Light. With that, I immediately jumped up out of a deep sleep and found that my face was covered with tears, just as in my dream. I have no question that this was a real visit from my friend Vince—a true vision to the gateway into the other side.

A Glimpse of Heaven

Often I am asked the question "What is it like in Heaven?" I can only answer that I don't know. I have only seen a small glimpse of the wonderful place they call Heaven. And from that small glimpse I can assure you that we have nothing to worry about and everything to look forward to. From what I have experienced, I believe that Heaven is a beautiful place where we meet up with others who have crossed over—a place with no fear, no anger, and no hate, just beauty, peace, and love.

The spirits or souls of our loved ones who have passed try to communicate with us in different ways. As I showed with Vince, they attempt to validate through dreams that they are with us and are okay. Although we may be in a dream state, I do not refer to these experiences as dreams. I call them visits from those on the other side. These happen to many of us. It is their way of assuring us that they are doing well in the afterlife.

Although many people do experience these validations through dreams, unfortunately not everyone does. This may be because we all have different patterns and states of sleep. Your mind reaches different levels when you're asleep. Some of us go into a dream state in which we remember our dreams very vividly. Some of us believe that we sleep so deeply that we do not actually dream. We all dream; we just don't remember. Those on the other side can reach us only if we are in a certain state. If we go beyond that state or do not reach it at all, they cannot get through to us.

Of course, every dream that you have about someone who has passed away isn't necessarily a true visit, but you will know when a true visit happens. You will not question it; you will feel it and you will just know. However, if you look too hard for meaningful dreams, you may miss other signs outside of dreams that are right in your face.

When Vince came to me in my dream, I "knew" it. The feeling, the sight, the tears when I awoke—all were his way of saying thank you and sharing something special with me. The gift for me was having the opportunity to get a glimpse of the other side and the beauty it has to offer.

CHAPTER 6

Expect the Unexpected

6

Expect the Unexpected

So far, I have explained some of the ways that our loved ones try to communicate and validate things for us in our daily life. I need to again stress that one should not look hard for these signs. Just allow them to come. When conducting my readings with clients, I always tell them to expect nothing but the unexpected. The only people who have come to me for readings and have left disappointed were the ones who expected a certain person in spirit to come through and to talk about one specific thing. You never know what signs you will get, just as I never know what or who may come through during a reading. Anyone can come through, even someone you least expect and do not know well, or even not at all.

A Wrong Turn

On my way to conducting a party for eight women in Alpha, New Jersey, I made a wrong turn that would end up being right, in a sense. I came to a traffic light at a dead end in the center of town. I needed to go left, and the directions were sitting on the seat next to me. For some odd reason, my mind and body decided to make a right at the light without telling me. So I found myself driving down a road in this tiny little town, knowing that I would have to turn around. What did I do that for? Ahead on the right was a big supermarket. I decided to turn around in the parking lot and go the way I should have gone in the first place. As I put on my right turn signal and made the turn, I caught a glimpse of a memorial of flowers and other objects. Someone surely had died there. I pulled over as if a magnet had pulled me to the spot. I felt the intense energy of a young man whom I felt was killed there on the corner. No sign told me that; it was just an overwhelming feeling. I continued on my way, arriving at the party a few minutes late.

The readings at the party went very well—at least the first two did. Then came the third reading. It was for a woman who had one thing in her mind. If her father did not come through with the specific thing she had in mind, then the reading would be no good and it was not her father. This woman's reading turned out to be intense. First, her grandmother came through very strong, with names and other specifics. But this woman didn't want to hear what Grandma had to say. She had a very negative attitude. When her father began to come through, she loosened up a little and seemed to listen. But she really didn't care what her father had to say either. Apparently, she said a little prayer beforehand asking him to mention something special that they shared, something specific that he had to mention during the reading. Her father had a good sense of humor, and it was clear that he liked to joke around. Anyway, she walked out disappointed and disgruntled because she didn't hear what she wanted to hear.

Next came a young girl, about 17. She had a cute smile and sat very nervously in a chair across from me. The reading began. She didn't know, but she was about to receive some very intense messages. I explained to her as I always do, that *anyone* from the spirit world can come through, whether you were close to them or not. Messages for this girl began coming through from a grandfather figure who felt familiar to me for some reason. The young girl recognized everything I was relaying to her from her grandfather. Tears slowly rolled down her face as she grabbed a tissue. Then her grandfather stepped aside and another energy started to come through.

A young man stepped forward to give me messages for the girl. First, he wanted me to mention that he had one sister, whose name was Denise. The young girl looked up at me with a tear in her eye and mentioned that Denise was her best friend—still living. Denise was supposed to have come to the party this evening. The young man then showed me that he had passed away in a car accident. He told me his name and the date that it happened. Then the vision came very clearly to me. The accident had happened at the place where I made the wrong turn. I explained this to the girl. It was important for the young man to be specific, and he wanted to pass the message to both his mother and sister that he was okay and that he made it to the other side. The girl reached for another tissue. The boy then thanked her and pulled back his energy.

The grandfather energy began to take over once again during this young girl's reading. Several more messages came through for her. But before her grandfather pulled back his energy, he had one last message. I remember it well.

"Your grandfather wants you to pass on a message to your mother. He says that he is your mother's father, is that correct?"

She whispered "yes."

"He is showing me a movie that he would like you to pass on to your mom. It looks like the Wizard of Oz. Do you understand why he would show me that?"

Another soft whisper, "No, not at all."

"Well he keeps showing me that movie, so he is pretty persistent about it. And he thanks you for passing that message as well."

Then her grandfather pulled back his energy, and the reading came to a close. The young girl wiped away a few more tears and then told me about the young man who came through.

"My friend Denise, who was supposes to be here today, had a brother who was killed in a car accident right where you described. Everything you told me about him is true. As far as my grandfather and the Wizard of Oz, I have no idea, but I'll tell my mother."

Then she thanked me, wiped away another tear, and left the room. Within a few minutes, I heard a commotion in the other room and a woman yelling, "Oh my God, I don't believe it, Oh my God!" Then the woman ran into the room where I was sitting.

Oh my God, not her again. Save me. It was the woman whom I read just before the young girl—the one who walked out in a huff because she didn't hear what she wanted to hear. She came storming in ranting and raving.

"Oh my God. Oh my God, Joseph, you will not believe this, you just won't believe it."

I'm sure I will, crazy lady, I thought.

She went on,

"Before I came here today I asked my father to come through with a specific message—a message telling me the exact movie we used to watch all the time while I was a kid growing up. I prayed and told him that if it was really him he had to tell me that."

I was thinking this woman was a bit off her rocker. She kept rambling on.

"You just read my daughter and she told me the message that my father wanted her to pass on to me. She told me that he mentioned the Wizard of Oz. I have to tell you I cannot believe you said that to her. That was the movie I watched all the time with my father growing up. It was our favorite movie, the one I prayed that he would mention. I just don't know why he didn't mention it when you were reading me."

As I said, the man had a good sense of humor.

I have been working as a medium for years, and I still don't know what to expect. In the reading I just explained, the young girl was a messenger. This happens all the time. You never know. Sometimes it makes my job a little more difficult. People sit in front of me thinking of the family and loved ones whom they would like to come through, and not someone they don't know. I once did a session at the home of a person whose neighbor a few doors away had a son who was killed in an automobile accident. The son came through even though no one there knew him, and the neighbor was not even present. However, they all knew of the accident. And so the young man came through hoping that someone would pass on his message.

An Ordinary Reading?

An unexpected thing happened during what I thought was a normal reading for my Aunt Fran. Several things came up that I personally was unaware of. I felt the younger energy of a female whose life was taken from her. She began coming through with her initials, then her birthday, and so on. I had no idea who was coming through until my aunt said her name. She began giving me messages pertaining to her family and others that she wanted to acknowledge and send love to. Then she hit me with the details.

The entire event played out before my eyes. This young woman was a passenger in a pick-up truck. Some guy was in the driver's seat—her boyfriend at the time. They were drinking heavily and began to argue. The argument got heated with some heavy language going back and forth. She threatened to get out and walk. He decided to give her a little help. Still driving at a speed of at least 50 miles per hour, this guy had a few choice words before reaching over to the passenger door, opening it, and pushing her out. She tried to hang on. Her feet were dangling on the ground alongside the pick-up. She screamed at him with more choice words. Then he swerved back and forth until she could no longer hang on and slid down to the hard pavement.

That's not all. The thug pulled over, turned around, and went back. He wasn't looking to see if she was okay. He went back to run her over and finish the job. I'm not sure exactly what happened after that; I only know what my aunt told me after this reading. The real message that she wanted to bring through was the fact that she was murdered. From what I have been told of the girl's death, it was supposed to have been an accident.

The "story" was that she and her boyfriend were driving in a pick-up truck when she supposedly decided to climb out of the speeding truck to go to the back cab. During her climb to the back of the truck, she slipped and fell onto the highway. At this point, she instantly met her death. This was the story that was told to my aunt. There is no doubt in my mind that the girl was murdered. I do know that there are many secrets, untold stories, and murders hidden on this plane. A scary thought.

Sometimes It's Fun

Expecting the unexpected is fun at times in my line of work. But at times it can be distracting—like the time a friend's father popped in to visit me in spirit while I was getting ready for work. While I was brushing my teeth, he came out of nowhere with a message to relay. The person who was to receive the message was the husband of a very close friend of mine. I had met the man who passed over a few times at family gatherings. He used to joke with me about being a psychic. So even though he had passed he didn't miss an opportunity to taunt me a little once again.

I didn't know anything about this man other than his name and that he had seemed to be in an awful lot of pain from his back and other problems. Unfortunately, he had taken his own life. His message was the same as most who taken their own lives—a message to apologize and admit their mistake and also to validate to us that they are doing well on the other side. So I called my friend's husband to give him the message.

"Hey, John, how's it going?"

"Not too bad, hanging in there, Joe."

"Okay, John, this is going to sound a little crazy, but I had to call you."

"Why?"

"Well, you know what I do and all, you know with the psychic stuff and connecting with the spirits."

"Yeah, go on."

"Your father came to me just a few minutes ago. I felt I needed to call you right away, even though I will now be late for work."

"That is really weird, Dude, I just walked in the door and I'm never home this early. Normally, you wouldn't catch me at this time."

"Well I have to tell you that your father is very sorry for what he did. He didn't come through making up excuses, but he said it was about the pain. He also mentioned multiple sclerosis. Did you know if he had MS?"

"No. But if he did, I'm sure I would know."

"I think he had it and hid it from everyone. He was also showing me a wheelchair. I'm not sure if he was trying to say he would end up in one."

"Wow, this is really freaking me out."

"Why?"

"Joe, my dad worked in a wheelchair factory."

"Wow, I didn't know that."

"Yeah, I know you didn't. That why it is so crazy."

Crazy, maybe, but not if you expect the unexpected.

Another unexpected incident happened during a reading for Jack, a former neighbor and landlord of the apartment building in Sergeantsville, New Jersey, where I used to live. Jack was very aware of my work as a psychic medium and a little spooked by it. I was surprised when he asked me one afternoon if I would come over and give a reading to one of his female friends. That evening I went to Jack's to meet his friend Cathy. Cathy and I went over to the table and sat while Jack sat in a chair off to the side away from us. First, I began explaining how the reading works so that Cathy would understand. Then I began the reading. Cathy's grandmother came through first with several messages and details of her passing. Then the unexpected:

"I'm getting the energy of what feels like a young man. Actually, I believe he may be a young boy.

He is not showing me what he looks like, but his energy is definitely younger. He keeps telling me the number 5 is significant.

I think his name may begin with a D or it is something like Dominick.

He is also mentioning something about the month of August and March 15.

Now he is showing me what looks like a mountainside with a beautiful scene. I don't know why but it looks as if he is showing me an orange.

He is telling me that he is okay and he is happy where he is now. He says it was an accident and no one should blame themselves."

I happened to look over at Jack and noticed tears rolling down his cheeks. He looked extremely shaken up when he turned to us and said:

"I can't believe it. I honestly cannot believe this is happening.

I had a little brother Nick. When he was five years old we were up in the mountains with our family. We were walking along a trail and it was a hot August afternoon. My brother dropped his orange on the ground and it rolled toward the edge of a very large cliff. He went after the orange and fell from the cliff and died. Everyone blamed themselves for what happened.

My own kids don't know about my brother. It's something I never talked about with anyone. Oh yeah, and March 15th is my birthday."

Jack received some assurance from his brother that he is still around, even though it was more than 50 years ago. This had to have helped Jack in many ways. A week later when I stopped at Jack's, there was an old antique-looking stuffed bear very nicely secured in a hand-made glass case to ensure its safety. I asked Jack about the bear. He told me, "That was my little brother's bear." This was a sure sign that the messages delivered that day brought some very long-awaited healing to a well-needed place.

My Turn to Be Surprised

Expecting the unexpected is something I experienced first-hand at the other end of a reading. Sometime during the winter of 2003, an advertisement on my cable network really caught my attention. It was for an upcoming pay-per-view event of a very well-known psychic medium. He advertised that he would be taking calls from viewers throughout the show. What a cool idea, I thought, as I marked the date on my calendar. How great it would be to call in and talk to him. What would he say? Would my mother come through? All these things kept running through my head for days before the event.

When the show day finally arrived, I connected my VCR to the television so I could record the event—just in case I got through on the phone. When the show began, I kept anxiously dialing and re-dialing the phone number that was shown, hoping to get more than a busy signal. Within about four minutes, I got through. A recording came on explaining that I had reached the correct number and my call would be taken in the order it was received. Suddenly my heart began to pound. Was it panic, nervousness, excitement? I was about to talk to this famous medium. What will he say? What messages will come through? Will he know that I do the same work? I had no specific reason for making the call. My mother is around me and I validate that for myself all the time. I only called to see what he had to say—nothing more. No expectations.

My nerves were showing. I began to look for my tape recorder and the attachment that I use to connect the recorder to the telephone, as I do for my telephone readings. I hooked up the recorder and sat smoking cigarette after cigarette with my finger poised over the record button. I got up a few times to make sure the VCR was recording. I was sweating and a nervous wreck.

I stayed on hold for over an hour, but I was still confident that my call would be taken. However, I noticed that the psychic medium was taking very few calls. I was under the impressions that the entire pay-per-view show would be directed toward callers. I was wrong. Lengthy clips of his tour were shown punctuated by the occasional call. I was becoming annoyed.

I paced, sat down, lit another cigarette, sat on the couch, back and forth, up and down. Eventually, the tour coverage came to an end and the psychic medium took another call. I listened in amazement at what he was telling the woman on the phone and at how well it was hitting home for her. Her reading ended and he took one more call. He began to explain the following to the caller.

"Please correct me if I'm wrong. But for some reason I believe this message is not for you. I believe it may be for someone who is on the phone now. Someone who is on hold waiting to get through to me. So if anything I'm saying does not make sense to you, I'm sorry. If it does make sense, then good it is for you. Just be sure to let me know."

Everything he said to this woman made no sense to her. She had no idea what he was talking about. On the other hand, it hit home real hard with me. He went on to say,

"I have the energy of a young man coming through.

I feel as if the letter V may be significant to his name.

He's telling me that he took his own life, using a gun.

The number 13 and the month of October are also important.

He is saying that this happened near his home in the woods.

He is showing me a large tree, so I feel that it happened near this tree.

He wants to thank someone for helping him with his crossing over.

Also for their help in supporting his family through the crisis.

He is also talking about a validation through a dream.

I'm not sure what he means by that, I think he is saying that he came to this person through a dream once before.

He also wants to mention that he has two sisters and would like them to receive the message also, if at all possible.

He thanks this person once again before pulling his energy back.

I'm sorry that this message was not intended for you and I do hope that the person on hold hears the message and is able to validate it for him or herself."

Then the show switched back to the tour. I sat stunned at the message that just came through. Then, I was overcome with excitement and jumped up and down, scaring my dog.

"I can't believe it. Vince came through. Holy Mary, Mother of God, I really can't believe it."

Everything the psychic medium said was completely accurate. The date was the anniversary of the day that Vince took his life. It all happened as he said, in the woods near the tree. The dream, the thank you, the two sisters—all matched perfectly. Not to mention the fact that I was the one on hold waiting. Vince was always a jokester, loved to make people laugh and loved to get into trouble. The two of us were well known for doing stupid stuff together in class that ended with us in the principal's office in big trouble. I can see him laughing at the way he blew my mind with his message. He may have thanked me, but I thank him many times over. He taught me so much from these experiences and validations.

I hung up the phone knowing that I received a reading without even talking to the medium. I never expected that—again, the unexpected.

If my mind had been at all closed or focused on hearing from a specific person with a specific message, then this experience and message would probably never have happened. Moreover, the message from Vince didn't come to me just because of my work as a medium. It happened because I was open to the experience. This is why it's important to keep an open mind and expect the *completely* unexpected.

CHAPTER 7

Bringing Validation

7

Bringing Validation

"Spirit works in strange ways."

I have used this quote for years and use it to this day. No need to elaborate. Still, many years into doing psychic work, I find that the quote proves itself over and over. What I'm saying is that we never know what to expect when it comes to our loved ones on the other side. The story here as well as many others throughout this book will help to prove that the quote I have been using for years is a true fact. We never know and unfortunately do not realize how the spirits work and how hard they try to prove their presence to us.

I am constantly surprised by the messages that spirits bring. What I stress to every client before I conduct a reading is to have an open mind. What they may expect to happen or want to happen usually never does. Moreover, a spirit often comes through who has no strong connection to the person I'm reading. So, why does a spirit with no connection to you come through? Keep in mind that spirits do not often have an opportunity to connect with their loved ones—usually not at all. Actually, they connect with us every day, but we fail to recognize or acknowledge the little signs they give us. Therefore, when a spirit sees an opportunity to connect, they do it, whether you know them or not. The spirits of those who passed over hope that somehow the message will be forwarded to their loved one.

Bill and Family

When I was in 10th grade, I met my buddy, Bill. We became like brothers—always together every day. We became a part of each other's family. When we were not seen together, everyone would ask where the other one was. Bill is to be the one person who can validate so many of the unbelievable psychic experiences I had throughout high school. He was a big skeptic and is now a big believer. I used to sit at his kitchen table and read Tarot cards for his entire family. Through the cards and my psychic feelings, I predicted their marriages, their future careers, and all their children.

Time passes and we meet new people and lose connections with old friends. But Bill was the only friend whom I continued to have contact with for many years after school. Eventually, I moved away and the contacts became rare. For a few years I didn't see Bill at all. Then, I was amazed to see Bill, his wife, and his immediate family at my mother's funeral service—a heartwarming thing for them to do. (We overruled my mother's wishes to have no memorial service, because we very much needed to give tribute to my mother.) Bill's mother Debbie said to me at the service,

"Remember that you will always have me as your mother; you have always been a son to me."

What a beautiful thing to say. Bill's family also made me feel bad that our connection had been lost for a short period. I called Bill a few times within the year after my mother's passing. Unfortunately, the connection ended once again for a few years. For a while, I thought that he didn't want to be bothered.

During this time period of about two years, I had begun to recognize my ability to communicate with spirit. I was driving back to my father's house in Levittown, I basically grew up. Out of nowhere, my thoughts were interrupted by the thought of Bill's mom. This was odd. Bill's mom—not Bill! I tried to ignore it but I couldn't stop thinking about her. Then, I kept thinking I should call her. But I told myself no and gave myself all kinds of excuses. What would I say? She'll think I'm crazy. I continued driving and tried to put the thought out of my mind. There was no chance of that. Maybe she had been thinking about me a lot lately. Yes, that was it. But then other thoughts popped into my head. Maybe someone passed away. Next, I got the whole feeling of whom. I was not sure if it was me or the reality that it was probably spirit giving me this information. Better yet, there seemed to be a woman in the car telling me to call. I also had the strange feeling that I knew the woman who was in the car with me at the time—if in fact there *was* a woman in the car with me.

One of the hard parts about being a psychic is that at times we cannot determine what's real and what's a vivid imagination. I had never thought that I could connect with spirit when I wasn't trying. That's why I tried to ignore the urgings. But the woman didn't give up. This made me realize that I had to make the call. If I didn't, she would not leave me alone.

After arriving at my father's house, I was driven to call Bill's mom, Debbie. I kept getting the answering machine, but I didn't want to leave a message. Finally, someone answered. It was Debbie. She had no idea who I was and I simply said "you have been thinking about me all day haven't you?" That was all I needed to say. She knew me right away simply because I was right. I began to tell her why I called. I asked if someone had passed away in the past few weeks or months. Then I described who I thought had passed. It turned out that I was right on about everything, including the person's name. I explained beforehand about how I connect with the other side. This is something I did not do back in the days of my reading for the family.

I mentioned that I knew I had to do a group reading for her and some other family members. I promised to call her in the next few days to set everything up. She stressed over and over that I'd better call. I pointed out that I had no choice; that's why I called in the first place. The call ended, but the day had not. Within less then 30 minutes I found myself knocking on Debbie's front door. Someone in spirit said I needed to show my presence. Just another mind-boggling experience for both of us, especially since the family members were all in the kitchen talking about me right before my arrival! I hung around for a little while sharing the experiences of my current life as a medium. Soon after, I went on my way with the promise that I would call Debbie within the week.

Again I found myself on the phone the next day seeing up the next possible date to get together. Earlier, I had told Debbie that it would be at least a few weeks before I would be available. I was surprised to find that this was not the case. I was able to set up a time within the next few days.

Family Session

The day of the reading arrived, and I looked forward to driving back to my home town and to help some very good friends and adopted family members connect with their loved ones. While I was listening to my car radio, Bill's sister, Kelly, popped into my mind. I thought that maybe she would come along to the group reading. Then I thought, why? It really didn't make sense. Her mother, grandmother, and aunt all wanted to connect with her grandfather whom she never even met. They wanted to connect with loved ones from way back. Most likely, these souls wouldn't mean a whole lot to her. Once again, I was proved wrong. She was there and she received messages.

I began the session with a long explanation of how everything works. I pointed out, as I always do, that no one should expect to connect with a specific person. This can lead to disappointment or make them blind to the messages they do receive. Another thing I stressed to everyone was the fact that it's possible that I may connect with another part of the family. For example, someone close to their husband, or even an ex-husband. I don't always stress this, but I felt I needed to at this time. I even mentioned to Bill's sister Kelly that she would probably not receive any messages from this session. I was way off. The entire session went in a direction that I couldn't have predicted.

The information that first came through didn't seem to click with anyone in the room. However, as it was coming through to *me*, it was very clear and extremely strong. This is my sign that the information pertains to someone in the group. After a few minutes, Kelly spoke up. "I know someone whose sister passed in that manner and with that name, but I didn't really know her." At this point I had to stress to everyone that our loved ones on the other side will take any opportunity they can to try to connect with those still living. I told Kelly that if this information seems to pertain only to her, then it was definitely a message for her. I have often experienced messages in which spirits not related or not even close came through to someone. This is mostly because they hope that the message will be carried to their loved ones. This was what happened with this particular spirit. Once Kelly became aware of the message, the spirit pulled away to allow another spirit to come through.

To everyone's amazement, my focus once again went to Kelly—the one person in the group whom I didn't think would have this experience. A young man came through very clearly. I was able to give such an accurate description that Kelly had no problem knowing who it was. It took her only a moment to catch on even though she never suspected this person would come through. The young man was her husband's brother who had passed on within recent years. Even though I have been a friend of the family, I never knew anything about this young man. He really wanted to make sure his message would be carried on to his family. Kelly was his only connection in doing this. He made sure she got the message by bringing through information that was just too accurate not to believe. He mentioned the fact that someone put a fishing pole in his casket during the service. She had no idea about the fishing pole. The following day she called me to confirm about the fishing pole. She also set up an appointment for her husband's family to have a reading.

I had had my own feelings about how the group session at Debbie's house would go. Just from knowing everyone so well, I figured that Debbie would get the most out of this session. To me, Bill's mom Debbie was the biggest believer and wanted this more than anyone. I also figured that Debbie's aunt who recently passed would be the first to come through, followed by her father. One of the first things that came through for Debbie was that there was indeed someone present who wanted to come through. This spirit let us know that he would come through last, just to throw us off.

The session continued with my energies being pulled toward Barbara (Kelly and Bill's aunt). First, her former mother-in-law came through. It took her a moment to figure out who it was. I went on to tell her that in the past she felt her mother-in-law didn't like her. The message was that she was wrong about her feelings. This is why her mother-in-law was coming through. She wanted her to know that she loved her like a daughter and she should realize this just because of her connecting. She also came through with the message that the person Barbara wanted to connect with was trying to come through. This person was a joker when he was alive, so why not on the other side? Another method for spirit to make sure we get the message.

Barbara began to receive a lot of information from her husband who had passed many years previously. Everything was very clear. To me, it seemed like a complete conversation, definitely a good emotional experience for her. At several points during this session, I was getting an unclear message pertaining to a seven-year-old girl. As with other messages, this would not leave my mind until someone recognized who it was. A couple of things were clear to me about this little girl. She was seven years old and I could see her on a "missing" poster. No one in the group had any idea whom I was talking about. The message was not very clear, I tried to analyze it by asking questions of the group. Did a friend ever have their little girl abducted? Was there ever a little girl missing in the area? A neighbor? A relative many years ago? Still nothing. Other information was coming through, but the little girl thing continued to come up.

About an hour into the reading, I began to get a name that wasn't very clear or recognizable. I tried repeatedly, but no one could fit the name with anyone past or present. Then I received a very clear message—the first of its kind. It was: "You're just not getting it, take a break." Wow. Spirit actually told me to take a break. At this point, I had received so much information, which came through stronger then usual, that my brain was cluttered and pretty far gone. I took the message seriously and stopped the session for a break, stressing to the group that this was a first.

After the break, I continued. There was no problem receiving the information. All messages came through clearly, as in the beginning of the session. The break was definitely a good idea. My focus went right to Bill's mother and grandmother. Still, every few minutes I focused back on Kelly or her Aunt Barbara. It was nothing like earlier; the messages were brief. I was getting odd pieces of information, such as the year 1955. No one could place that year. Every now and then, I would get the little girl coming through. Also, a health warning came through. The message was to tell the group that someone had to be careful of their heart. This was not a warning of death. Usually, this type of warning is to *prevent* future health problems, such as heart surgery. I told them that a person in the family tree has heart disease. All they need to do is exercise and watch the diet. Unfortunately, it was not the person they all thought it was.

The grandmother in the family wanted to ask a question of her late husband. I let her know that in most cases they don't answer. She wanted to know if I would bring through the nickname that her husband called her. To my surprise, I did receive some information about this. Generally, spirit shows me things that make sense to *me* so I can interpret the information correctly. Anyway, I began to see several Disney movies. Then I was told that I would not get the name because I was not at all familiar with the movie and the name. Then her daughter knew the answer almost instantly. The nickname was the name of the Disney movie Lilo and Stitch, with which I wasn't familiar. So she received her answer, the nickname was Stitch.

One thing that I found amazing was the information I received for my friend's mother Debbie. I have known Debbie for many years. She has always had a strong interest in the subject of psychics and ghosts. At one time we even went together to a few different readers. Debbie seemed to want this session very much. I couldn't believe the information I was receiving. Because I know Debbie so well, I identified the information I was receiving with anyone in the room but her. I was told that she had come to the conclusion that there was no heaven or afterlife. This was mostly because her father never showed her any signs that he was around. She believed that he would have if it was at all possible. Since she didn't acknowledge any of her father's signs, she became a nonbeliever. The sad thing is that we all get signs all the time. We just don't see them as such, or we disregard them. Sometimes we just look too hard. I know this from my own experience with my mother's passing. Along with this and much more information from Debbie's father about anniversary dates, birthdays, and nicknames, I would say that she now believes.

After the family's session, I could see that everyone had a great experience except Debbie. I told her that of all the people I know I would never expect this from her. It was just too much information not to believe. Her father even mentioned to look for another validation in the coming weeks. He also knew. This happens often in my readings. Spirit loves to show signs after the reading, just to make sure people get it.

The sad thing about this session is the heart message or warning that came through. I recall that all of us mentioned to the grandmother that she was breathing heavily. She put it off as her normal breathing pattern. I even said that it was a little odd, especially for a nonsmoker. A few days later, she had congested heart failure and ended up in intensive care. After a week in the hospital, she was sent home and has been fine since. This upset me for another reason that I kept to myself. The day I thought about Debbie and calling her I had another thought. I felt that someone may have passed, but I was not really sure. At this time I thought of the grandmother and wondered if it could have been her. I wish I had remembered this during the reading. Maybe I could have put the pieces together. And maybe the warning really was about the grandmother and that her problem was not preventable. Spirit does work in strange ways.

Missing Girl

As I headed back home, much of the information had left my mind. After most readings, I lose a lot of the information. However, parts of this session did stick with me. After getting home, I had a little visit. While sitting at my computer and checking my e-mail, the seven-year-old-girl came to my mind. After a few minutes I discovered that she was not in my mind, that her spirit had come home with me. I discovered that she had nothing to do with the group session. I believe she attached to me when

I was driving through the lake area. I received all kinds of information, along with seeing her completely clearly. I came to believe that she is in the lake. She was abducted, murdered, and dumped there. I had even received a clear view of the man who did it. This was just too much information to ignore. With that I searched until the early morning hours trying to find her face on missing children websites. I found nothing and I tried everything I could think of to no avail. I believe that the 1955 message most likely pertained to the little girl. This would make sense if I could find some information. So, I'll continue to search because I can't get her out of my mind. I hope I can get a validation on this and can help her. I always wanted to help with missing children if the opportunity came. I know eventually I will figure this out, but it could take some time.

CHAPTER 8

Turning It On and Off

8

Turning It On and Off

Again and again people walk up to me and ask me to "read" them. Sometimes a friend says, "tell me something"; other times it's a complete stranger. If being an auto mechanic were my profession, would you say "fix my car?" Still, people are people.

In the middle of a conversation at a bar where I worked, a person might turn and ask me what I do for work and when I say I'm a psychic medium, they first respond with a laugh. Most people don't believe me at first. They think it's a joke. Sometimes I start the joke by whispering, "I see dead people." They always respond with laughter but say, "no, seriously, what do you do?" Then I tell them I'm a psychic medium, and still they don't believe it. When finally convinced, most turn to me and say "well then tell me something." They think it's a game.

It simply doesn't work that way. I'm often asked, "What do you do when you're out shopping or something?" Well I do shop, and I don't think about being a psychic 24 hours a day. Most of the time I'm able to turn my connection with spirits off and on. Before I do a reading for a client, I spend twenty to forty minutes in meditation and prayer. This is my way of turning it on, or "tuning in" to the spiritual realm. When I'm complete with my work, I end with another prayer of thanks and a short meditation—my way of turning it off.

So when someone comes up to me and wants me to tell them something, unless I'm in tune, as I like to put it, there's not much I can say except "have a nice day." Okay, I've said that. But there are always exceptions. I may be standing in line at the grocery store and have a strong urge to tell the woman behind me that her mother is with her and sends love. It actually has happened, but I never said a word to the person. I wanted to, but just couldn't bring myself to do it. I wouldn't want the person to break down in the middle of the store, or, more likely, to think I am a nut. I could end up getting arrested. So in these rare cases, I keep it to myself.

Uninvited Visions

I try to stress to people that being a psychic does not have all the benefits that one would think. Still, things occasionally come to me out of the blue when I'm not in tune with my work. One night many years ago when I was still with my ex, I was visiting my aunt in New Jersey. Aunt Fran and I were sitting at her kitchen table drinking coffee and talking at about 11 pm. I suddenly jumped up and just knew my ex was in bed at that exact moment with someone else. My aunt laughed at first and said I was overreacting. Over and over I called, and then the cell phone. No answer the entire night. The next day, I found out I was completely correct. The psychic instinct that came out of nowhere helped me put an end to a relationship that should have ended many years earlier.

Another thing that bothers me is when I tell people what I do and they respond with, "then what am I thinking?" I said that I'm a psychic. Did I mention that I am a mind reader? I wish I could read minds. Then right now I would be sitting at the casino reading the dealer's mind and winning a whole lot of cash. I have the gift of being able to communicate with spirits and predict future events.

For a long time I felt that my ex was up to no good. Tuning into it for myself seemed impossible. Part of me felt there was cheating going on; the other part of me thought it was my own insecurity. Finding the truth seemed to be such a far reach. Then one day in my aunt's kitchen, the answer came to me out of the blue. It was not the answer or message that I wanted, but I'm glad it came. I believe a spirit was helping me to make the change that I needed to make in my life. Spirit also knew that this was the one real thing I needed to make the right change.

When information comes to me unexpectedly, I know that it is spirit reaching out to me for some reason. Many things have come to me over the years—some I can't do anything about. For example, when I was in my early teens, I kept getting visions of a major earthquake. Some days I had a feeling as if the earth were shaking under my feet. I got a vision of an earthquake, which I was sure would hit in my home area. It did hit, but not in my area. It ended up being the biggest quake in Los Angeles, California.

Many other visions came to me throughout my life. Once I saw visions of a plane crashing. It seemed to crash in a populated area, and people who were on the ground would also be killed. I felt that there was someone very famous on the plane, such as the President. I thought this because I had more visions of a funeral that looked to me like the biggest funeral of all time. An event that would have a severe impact on the entire nation.

After seeing these visions on and off for about a week, I began telling friends and people around me at work. Often when I fail to tell anyone of my visions, something happens. This time I had it all covered. Within a few weeks a well-known singer-actress Aaliyah died when her plane crashed. Friends called me asking if this was the vision I was getting. No, it was not. She is famous, but this crash is killing many, and the funeral is the biggest ever, in all of history. Within one more week, the visions came to life. I saw the plane that crashed into the Twin Tower in New York City on September 11. That vision of 9/11 was the most intense vision I've had that had come to full life, and it would have the most impact.

A few years after the 9/11 vision, another unusual vision came to pass. It was a very mixed message and a vision that I received over a period of about two weeks. I kept getting the date August 14. I knew something major was going to happen on that day, but I wasn't sure what. I also had the sense of an earthquake. So trying to put it all together, I came to my own conclusion.

I decided that an earthquake would be hitting on August 14. I had the feeling that the only problem was that it would be a big deal, but I was not feeling that it would be real bad—no real bad vibes as with the plane crash visions. Within a week of having this vision, which was well before August 14, I felt that a small earthquake would occur in, of all places, my own town. I lived outside Milford, New Jersey. And I felt the earth move under my feet alright—something that just does not happen where I live—especially in New Jersey. But it happened.

No one was injured and no major disaster came from the quake. Still, I wondered what happened with the whole date mix-up? I was still getting feelings about August 14th. As it turned out, I was away on vacation when I heard on the news that the United States was experiencing that largest blackout in United States history, and it was August 14.

Actually, both visions were correct; I just put them together wrong. There was an earthquake, and the August 14 power outage proved to a national event that would impact many lives.

Having visions and being a psychic do not necessarily work to my benefit. If spirit wants me to know something, they tell me, and if I or anyone is not meant to know something, then we shall never know. If it worked for me, I would have known my mother was going to pass. Maybe I could have prevented it. If only she had gotten to the hospital in time. If only I had been in tune enough to see this. Again, even if I did, it was all meant to be—no matter how young, how old, how good, how bad, how ugly, or how cute—when your time is up, it's up. It's all a part of the Lord's plan.

Sometimes words just come spewing from my mouth. Once a 16-year-old girl said to me with a cocky attitude "if you're so psychic then tell me something." I blurted out, "You're pregnant, go to the doctor." The girl's mouth fell open. She really had no response except to deny that I was correct and say that I was no psychic. Several days later she came back to apologize for her attitude and skepticism and to let me know that she had come to find out that she was pregnant.

On the other hand, even though I could very well tell people something when they ask, I choose not to. I take my work with the spirit realm very seriously. To me it's not a joke, and I'm not here to tell you something just because you found out two seconds ago that I'm a psychic. Since I do take my work seriously, I do my own preparations beforehand—like my prayer and meditation. Even though this is my way of opening up to the energies, the energies and the ability to communicate are always there.

Validation and Re-validation

My partner Bob likes to ask me from time to time to do something "magical"—meaning to give him a reading, even though he knows I'm not comfortable about reading those close to me. I know a little too much about him. Bob's father passed of lung cancer several years ago, so I know that he wants to hear from his father. To me it's hard with someone I know well because I tend to feel as if I'm not going to say anything significant enough. I did read him, his mother, and two sisters when we first met and when I didn't know anything about his family. But now I know, and this evokes my fear that nothing will come through clearly.

One night while relaxing on the couch and watching television, Bob was about to get a message of his own. He turned to me and said,

"Let's do something magical."

"Magical, like what? A reading?"

Of course, I knew what he was hinting at, but I was in no mood what-soever. I was completely relaxed watching TV—it just wasn't happening. "Sorry, Bob." But within only a few minutes there was a strong presence in the room standing next to us on the couch. I was getting a vision of Bob's father standing there in front of us. He gave me a message to pass on to his son. It sounded crazy to me, but I passed it on.

"Hey, your dad's favorite Star Trek character was Doctor Spock, right?" I asked.

"What?"

"What was your dad's favorite Star Trek character? Was it Doctor Spock?"

"I don't know, why?"

"Well, I think your dad's here and he is telling me that Doctor Spock is his favorite Star Trek character."

"Yeah, right."

"Seriously, that's what he is saying and he is saying it for a reason.

"Why would he say that?"

"I have no idea. Maybe it is a validation that you need to check."

So Bob phoned his mother to ask if she knew what his father's favorite Star Trek character was. She said she was not too sure but thought that it was Doctor Spock. With that, he hung up the phone, and that was pretty much the end of it for then. We continued to watch television. The show was "Wife Swap." In this show, two families swap wives for a week, and each wife lives out the other wife's daily routine. This show was about to have a big impact on the evening.

One of the wives was about to throw a little party for the other wife's husband—a little something to show him that someone cares. The husband just so happened to be very much into computers, as was Bob's fa-ther. The husband also happened to be a huge fan of Star Trek. When the husband arrived home, he certainly was surprised—especially since all of the guests were wearing a special prop of his favorite Star Trek Character. They were all wearing Doctor Spock's pointy elf-like ears.

At that moment, the husband wasn't the only one surprised. Bob and I sat on the couch looking at each other in amazement. This was definitely a sign from Bob's father. Bob's mother even confirmed by checking with his aunt, that Spock was indeed his favorite Star Trek character. This was not the only message Bob would receive from his father. Within the next week or so, his father made it very clear that he was present.

Getting ready to retire for the evening, we headed to the bedroom. Nothing seemed out of the ordinary at first. We both happened to be looking in the same direction when someone walked past our bed and into our bedroom, then disappeared. It was the full-figure shadow of a man. It was not a shadow on the wall. It was a person, but I didn't see who it was. I only felt that the energy was that of a man. Bob saw it, too. Scared the heck out of Bob, because he had never seen a spirit before. But I communicate with spirits. They talk to me, I hear them, I feel them, but not often do I see them, especially walking through my bedroom. The appearance of this spirit spooked me at first. He would not identify himself to me. He only let me know that he was a male. Bob, on the other hand, was totally spooked. "Who was that? What was that? He pulled the covers over his head to hide. "Is it still here?" All I could do was laugh; it was spooky, but funny, too.

Bob was getting a taste of what it's like for me at times. But who was it? My feelings are that this was just another message for Bob from his father. The only time one can see a spirit is when that spirit wants to be seen. I know from my own experience that this is true. When I do readings for others and visually see the spirits, they want me to see them so that I can describe them. But I don't always see them. The spirit that walked through our bedroom definitely wanted Bob to see him but didn't want me to know who he was. Why? Probably because he knew that I would know, but he wanted his son to validate it and appreciate it on his own.

Sometimes our loved ones like to re-validate the messages they sent us previously, especially when we question whether their message really was a sign from the other side. It's best never to question whether or not it's a sign. Just validate it as being a sign and appreciate the sign you receive. From doing my work for many years now, I find that spirit likes to give us a second sign or validation. They want us to know for sure who it is and that they are with us and watching over us.

I tell my clients that something I say now may not have happened but may soon happen as a re-validation from their loved ones who have passed. For example, while doing a reading for a client, I found that her father was very adamant about re-validating a previous message from him. I explained to her:

"Your father is telling me that he just visited you recently."

"Yes, Joseph, I believe he may have."

"Well, he is telling me that he heard you talking to him and singing while you were cleaning the house."

"I talk to him all the time."

"He is mentioning a picture on the wall above the stairs of someone in a uniform. He is telling me that he is the one who keeps knocking the picture down."

"Oh my God, Joseph. I knew it. I knew it was my father knocking down the picture. I was just talking to him the other day, and then his military picture fell off the wall. The picture hangs right above the stairs."

This was a simple way for this woman's father to validate again that he was the one knocking down the picture. As I keep saying, one should not necessarily look for a validation or a re-validation. Instead, allow the validation to come to you.

Pay attention to all things that just come to you. Maybe there was a day you were running late but felt as if you shouldn't leave at that moment. Then you later find out that there was a bad accident blocking your route. It could have been you in the accident if you left a little earlier.

Learning to trust yourself and the things that come to you is important. I have learned this in giving messages to my clients, friends, and family—things that sound crazy or bizarre to me, but are indeed messages. These messages are from our loved ones on the other side as well as from the guardian angels that watch over us every day.

CHAPTER 9

Blaming Yourself

9

Blaming Yourself

Death is hard enough to deal with, but it is especially hard when we have issues around a loved one's passing. These issues leave us stuck, dealing with the guilt that perhaps we could have prevented the person's death. For example, maybe you believe that Uncle Charlie on the other side is mad at you for not getting to the hospital to see him before he passed away. Or, maybe you believe that your father hated his funeral and the way you had prepared it. Or, perhaps you didn't even show up at your cousin Edward's funeral. We hold so many things inside when dealing with a person's death. We need to let go of these things. No soul on the other side is mad or upset with us in any way. That's not the way it is over there.

The other side is a beautiful place where all our loved ones meet up. It is a place with no negative emotions like the ones we have to deal with on this plane. Our loved ones who have passed want us to be happy and to live out our life here the best we can, never reflecting on the negative things, but only the fun and positive times we have spent together. I have learned these things myself through my readings and work as a medium.

Healing Lives

I like to refer to a medium as a doctor whom many of us need, but never go to see. Healing is a major part of the work I do—emotional healing. Many of us need this healing but sometimes repress so much emotion that we don't even realize it.

Communicating with spirits on the other side has taught me much about dealing with death. Besides giving validation to those who need it, I receive messages of medical advice that is also helpful, sometimes pointing out such illnesses as diabetes or heart trouble. In my years of doing this work, I didn't realize that I could be instrumental in saving lives as well. This became clear one day in March 2006, when I came across one of the most difficult clients I've had.

Reluctant Client

Karen had set up an appointment for 1 pm in the afternoon. At 12:55, she called saying she was lost. Luckily, Karen was on my street just three lights away. I told her that she needed to turn around and come back in the opposite direction. Easy. She should arrive within the next few minutes. Twenty minutes later and no Karen. Usually before an appointment, I start to feel a presence of some sort and sometimes even receive messages ahead of time. However, at this point I wasn't feeling anything at all. 1:20 pm and still no Karen. I thought maybe she had changed her mind. Sometimes people are afraid of what they might hear through me, afraid that someone will come through and be mad at them or tell them something they don't want to hear.

At about 1:30, there was a knock on my door. It was Karen. As I opened the door, I felt an overwhelming energy around her that didn't feel good at all. I let her know that I was upset with her for showing up 35 minutes after her call. Karen didn't seem to care. I received nothing but an "attitude" from her. I had the feeling that she really didn't want to be here. When I asked her how she had heard of me, she responded in a negative manner and told me that I should figure it out on my own. I began to dislike this woman and dreaded the reading.

We went into the room where do I readings and sat down across from each other. I asked her if she was familiar with any well-known mediums. The first well-known medium's name I mentioned brought on more of a negative attitude, and she said to me:

"Yeah he's a crock, it's all a bunch of shit."

"What do you mean?"

"I think it's all a bunch of crap, I don't believe in any of it."

"Then what are you doing here?"

"A friend told me that I needed to see you, that it would be good for me."

"Well then you need to open your mind and listen to what comes through for you."

I was thinking to myself, if you don't want to be here, then leave, darn it. I began to explain how the reading works, as I do at the beginning of all my readings. Karen kept huffing and puffing in an annoyed manner. She was not comfortable with my doing this reading. I stopped the tape recording because I was getting annoyed.

"Look if you don't want to be here, maybe you should leave. I take my work seriously and apparently you do not. So you are more than welcome to just go if that is what you want."

"No, I want to do it, so go on."

I pressed "record" and once again explained how the reading works. More negative attitude and negative energy. Karen built a wall to block out any energies that wanted to come through. Obviously, there was something that she didn't want to hear or face. Even though *she* kept trying to block out the energies, they began to connect with *me*. Her mother started to come through. Everything from her name to the date of her death was mentioned. Karen really began to make me mad.

"You're very general" she said.

"Excuse me?"

"That could be anyone, which is very generalized."

"That is just your opinion at this time; why don't you just listen?"

If they can get mad on the other side, which they don't, I think Karen's mom would have been real angry by this time. So much real information came through from her mother and from others. Everything I was telling Karen made perfect sense, but it was not good enough for her. Suddenly, another energy came through and took over the reading. Karen was about to get a real quick attitude adjustment, but not from me.

"Your mother is telling me that she has a younger man with her. He is pointing to his head and telling me that is what caused his passing. He keeps saying 'son.' So he must be your mother's son or your son. He is saying that the 23rd of a month is important to him, and I believe he is saying that his name is Freddy."

Karen totally lost it—an outpouring of emotions and tears. She put her head into the chair pillow and began crying heavily and shaking as if she were having a nervous breakdown.

"Oh my God, oh my God," she said. "Is it really him? Is he really telling you this? Please tell me the truth. Please tell me this is really him."

"Yes, it is really him, I couldn't make this up, could I?"

"No, please tell me more," she pleaded.

"He keeps mentioning 23 to me and is showing me guns. Either he collected guns or maybe he was shot. He is telling me to tell you that he is sorry, but it was an accident. He says he didn't leave anything behind—no note or message. He says that is because it was an accident. He says he is with your mother, Ann. He wants you to let Dad know, too, that he is ok. Freddy is happy on the other side and wants you and Dad to be happy. Your relationship has been falling apart since his death. That is not what he wants to see happen. He also wants to send love to his two sisters.

He says happy birthday, meaning that he passed around the time someone's birthday. Enjoy your birthday; don't reflect on me passing around that time. From this point on, he says that things will get better and that you should play this tape for your husband to listen to also. No one could have prevented this from happening; it was an accident."

The reading came to an end and Karen was pretty shaken up. We got up from our seats, and I gave Karen a well-needed hug. This brought even more of her emotions to the surface. As we walked into my living room, she told me the story about her son's death.

"My son Freddy was a very kind and warm-hearted person. He would stop on the highway and help injured animals, even if he ended up hours late for something. He was very caring. He loved to hunt and had several guns, which he cleaned often. Everything was going well for him; he had just purchased a new home in a wooded area so he could hunt.

Freddy died on the 23rd of the month and was found in his own backyard sitting on the tailgate of his truck with a gunshot to his head. The police said it was a suicide, even though he left no note. I know he would not have done that; we thought it was an accident. He broke his right arm and that was the hand he used to hunt. I believe he was cleaning his gun, and it accidentally went off in his face. The things that he used to clean the guns were on the tailgate next to him.

You were able to validate for me that it was an accident, Joseph. Thank you so much."

When I opened the door for Karen to walk out, she turned and said something very shocking.

"Joseph, I have to thank you once again. I will be around a lot longer now."

"What do you mean?"

"I have to be honest with you, Joseph. I was going to do myself in this week. I felt as if my son needed me to care for him on the other side, and the only way for me to accomplish this would be to take my own life as I thought he did. You validated that he is okay and my mother is taking care of him. Now I have no reason to kill myself."

Wow. After this, I came to realize that my work as a medium has more healing effects than I had ever imagined. Although my work may be healing for many who are touched by the experience, there are still those who do not receive or accept the healing that is there for them.

Accidents Happen

Here is another case of young man passing away in the most mind-boggling way. A gentleman I will call Don had come to see me for a private reading. His son came through during the session—a very handsome young man with a great sense of humor. His name was Jason. Jason said he was 22 years old when he passed away. He came through with great energy and full of jokes and humor. When the messages came through about how he passed, my mind went into a whirl.

Jason and a few of his good friends decided to go on a mud-flinging bah-ha adventure in his four-by-four truck. The adventure through the mud was going well until they ended up tire deep in mud in a little swamp that Jason and his friends thought they would be able to plow right through. The mud was up to the top of the tires and water was up to the bumper. There was no getting out of there without being pulled out by another truck.

Jason decided to give his father a call and let him know the situation, even though he knew he would get hell from his father for being in such a predicament. Jason's father agreed to help, and he headed out with his truck to pull his son out of the swamp. Meanwhile, Jason and his friends sat anxiously waiting. To pass the time, Jason decided to crawl out the back window of the truck so he could get the chain ready for when his dad arrived. This way he would only have to hook the other end of the chain to his father's pick-up truck.

With the truck still running, Jason leaned over the back end of the truck to hook the chain to the rear bumper. In less than a minute, Jason seemed to pass out. At this point, his father arrived to find his son leaning over the back of his truck. Before anyone could respond, Jason was dead. It took less then one minute. The exhaust pipe leading from the back of the truck was submerged in water, which intensified the amount of carbon monoxide. Jason breathed it in and had no chance whatsoever. He couldn't have known this. If the exhaust pipe were not submerged in water, this tragedy might not have happened.

Even though Jason was such a young soul in this life, it was his time. What he needed to learn in this life was complete. Now there is more work for him on the other side. You can imagine the pain that Jason's father and his friends were going through. The constant thought of "what if?" "What if we didn't go that day?" "What if I had gotten there a minute sooner?" "What if we didn't let him crawl out that window?" There should be no questioning or blame. It was just meant to be.

There is a reason for this that only God can explain. So if you are a person left behind by someone who has taken their own life or died in some tragic way, please come to learn that you could not have prevented it from happening. The person has crossed over to the other side and is happy there. Know that those who have passed want nothing more than to see us happy living our life until God chooses us.

My Blame Game

Not only do we blame ourselves for not being able to prevent someone's death, we blame ourselves for missing funerals and not seeing someone before he or she passes. During my readings I often find that my clients are tormenting themselves because they didn't go to see a close loved one just before they passed. This is something your loved one would want you to move on from. I always stress that there is no anger on the other side. They couldn't be mad at you even if they tried. There is no negative energy on the other side.

Being a medium does not exempt me from feelings of blame and guilt. Several years ago. my cousin Michael passed away suddenly at the age of 38. Michael had Rocky Mountain spotted fever from a tic bite that he got when we were kids. This led to a life of medical problems that doctors could not pinpoint. When his doctor changed his medication, Michael passed away that evening.

Michael had been living in Florida. At that point in my life, I just couldn't get there for the funeral. This began to disturb me to the point that I was constantly dwelling on it, thinking that he would be mad or upset that I didn't show up at his funeral. This really tormented me. Then Michael decided to send me a message to let me know that I didn't need to go to the funeral to see him.

Keep in mind that I don't always "see" spirits. I communicate with them in several ways, such as feeling and sound. On occasion I do see them.

This was one of those occasions. While I was cleaning my house thinking about not going to Michael's funeral, I turned and I saw this big guy in a white Tee-shirt smiling at me. I literally jumped and yelled—it scared me so much. I thought someone sneaked into my house. As soon as I jumped, he disappeared. I started to laugh. "Damn it, Michael, you scared me to death!"

Michael was a top wrestler and a very big guy. He was 6 feet 4 and about 350 pounds—big enough to put a scare into anyone. I really wanted to go to the funeral and pay my last respects, but my cousin Michael came to me instead.

Prayer Works

Perhaps someone close to you was very sick. You spend every day praying and having faith that your prayers will bring well-needed healing to your sick loved one. As time passes, your days are filled with increasingly more prayer as you pray for a miracle. Then the news comes that the person has passed away. You blame God for not answering your prayers. You begin to lose faith and believe that if there were a God he would have answered your prayers and not taken your loved one away from you. Now you are numb and stuck with no faith in prayer to carry you forward. I have found this to be a common emotional situation among many of my clients through the years.

We do not always get what we want, and we shouldn't expect it. Look at it his way: Your prayers did work, just not in the way you wished and hoped for. Your prayers helped your loved one to get to where he or she needed to be—crossing to the other side.

Prayer and faith both matter. As a part of my routine before I conduct my work, I depend on prayer. I pray giving thanks ahead of time and ask the spirits to come through clearly and accurately. This is my way of opening the channel, so to speak. When I'm finished my work, again I depend on prayer. It's my way of closing the channel and thanking the spirits for connecting with me. I pray that the spirits who come through make it safely to the other side and that those people for whom I have done readings receive the healing that they need. Prayer works, and having faith works also.

CHAPTER 10

Working in Heaven

10

Working in Heaven

Is there a Heaven? What is it like on the other side? What do they do there? Are my loved ones mad at me? Do they see what we are doing here?

There *is* a place where we all go when our outer bodies pass away. We all have a soul that eventually crosses over to the other side. It is a beautiful place without hate, anger, or negative emotions—a place full of love, light, and happiness. Our souls linger here on earth for some time after our passing. Therefore, yes, those who have passed are quite aware of the things that are going on with us here on earth. They are aware of the births of new children, the difficult times we face, and pretty much anything else they want to know about our lives here. They try to comfort us with their energies. We may not realize it at all, but they are there and they try very hard to let us know.

Heavenly Setup

There are different levels on the other side that are set up like a school—first through twelfth grades. Souls on higher levels are more able to communicate with us on earth; souls on lower levels may have a difficult time trying to communicate. There are reasons for the different levels: We live many lives throughout thousands of years. Each life is a learning experience for our souls. If you do not learn the lessons you came to this plane to learn, not only do you come back to do it again, you most likely will return to the same level on the other side from where you originally left.

Those who cause harm and pain to others end up flunking out of their grade. Not only will they return to the same plane on the other side, they may even go down a level or two—like repeating a grade.

Do I believe in Purgatory? Since I was raised Catholic, you would think so. But I do not believe such a place exists. Still, your soul should and will pay the price for doing wrong on earth.

When you cross over to the other side, you are greeted by one or more loved ones who have already crossed over. Then comes the big party they throw for you, were you meet up with hundreds of souls gathered to celebrate your arrival—souls whom you have known throughout your previous life on earth and also from many past lives. This is the time to celebrate your accomplishments you achieved on earth and your spiritual lessons. It is a time to catch up with the souls you have not seen for some time. From the party, you are led to the Council, as it is sometimes referred to.

The Council is like a Supreme Court. A group of very old and very wise souls discuss the things you have and have not accomplished on earth. An agreement is made between you and the Council as to where your soul shall go from there—to move to a higher level or to do work assigned by the wise Council. These facts I have learned from my experiences as a medium, from reading other experience, and through hypnosis and past life regressions.

Jimmy and the Angels

Children are very intuitive when it comes to spiritual things. When my nephew was a toddler of about 2 years old and just starting to talk (this is a good time to ask your own child questions). I sat down to ask him some questions.

"Jimmy, where were you before you were here?"

He looked puzzled at first. Then he put on a big smile and pointed upward. That was not enough for me, so I asked him again.

"Jimmy, where were you before you were here with Mommy and Daddy?"

Jimmy looked me right in the eyes and said "I was up there Uncle Joe, up there with the angels."

My nephew had no clue at that time what an angel was. He was not raised around religion or anything angel-related. I asked him another question.

"Jimmy, where were you before you were up there with the angels?" A quick reply came. I was down here with you, Uncle Joe. Down here a very long time ago."

Then Jimmy ran off to play and I sat in a daze for a moment. He answered my questions, for sure.

Souls of a Feather

As far as what our souls actually *do* on the other side, it varies from soul to soul.

When conducting readings, I find that it is common for souls who have taken their own lives to come through together on the same plane. This tells me that those who take their own lives end up together on the same level. This is not a bad thing. It is most likely a level at which all those souls need to learn. I find that those who pass on at a young age in a tragic way like a car accident also come through on the same level. It may be a different level, but it has in common another lesson that needs to be learned.

My Friend Matthew

I have not learned exactly what all souls do on the other side or what lessons they need to learn. But there is "work" for them to do. Whether or not this is assigned work—I don't know. What I have learned is that some souls take on some very intense work. I learned this from a very intense and interesting reading. This shows not only what some souls go on to do on the other side, but also how misdirected our justice system and politicians really are.

One day, a woman named Brenda came to see me for a private reading. Nothing seemed out of the ordinary before we began, although I sensed some deep suffering around her. The reading started out a little foggy, so to speak—meaning that things were not coming through clearly at first. Perhaps the first energy to come through was not necessarily the person Brenda wanted to hear from. In about 10 minutes, a young man stepped forth to connect with me and Brenda.

The young man said his name was Matthew, and he began showing me very vivid images to make sure the messages would come through clearly and accurately for Brenda. He kept saying Mom and sending love to "Mom." Matthew was Brenda's son. Matt went on bringing through to me the dates of his birthday, his passing, and other important dates. Then Matt acknowledged his sister, two brothers, and father by name. Tears began rolling down Brenda's cheeks, and I was overwhelmed with the emotional energy in the room. However, the reading with Brenda became even more interesting.

Matt went on to show me images and a complete description of what happened to him that horrible evening when his life was taken from him.

I explained to Brenda what Matt was showing me, and she confirmed each thing as we went along.

"Matt is talking about October and wants you to acknowledge it."

"Matt was killed in October."

"Matt is showing me a gun, and I hear two shots being fired as he shows it to me. Do you know what he is talking about, Brenda?"

"The guy who shot Matt fired two shots; one hit Matt in the back and the other hit his friend."

"Now he is giving me the name Mike and showing me a Wawa convenience store sign. Matt is also talking about a yellow Mustang."

"Mike is Matt's friend who was also shot that night and survived. A guy in a yellow Mustang did the shooting, and it all happened in the parking lot of Wawa."

Matt went on and on bringing more details to the surface for his mother, Brenda. Here is what happened:

One night Matt and a few of his friends, mostly girls, went for a walk to the store to pick up some cigarettes. As they walked into the store's parking lot, a man coming out of the store said some offensive things to one of the girls. Matt, the type of guy, who stands up for girls, said a few choice words of his own to the man. It became a shouting match. The man opened the car door of his yellow Mustang as if he were getting in to drive away. Matt and his friends continued to head into the store for cigarettes. As they walked toward the store, two shots fired out, and Matthew and one of his friends fell to the ground. Matt was shot in the center of his back and his friend was hit in the shoulder from behind. The man did not even hesitate and just got back into his car. Then police arrived. Matt did not survive his gunshot wound and passed away en route to the hospital. The man was arrested and taken away.

That was my first experience communicating with Matthew. He and I would connect again several times over the next year. Most of his family and friends have come to me hoping to connect with Matt. Each time, Matt has come through clear as a bell with his outgoing and fun personality. He even hung around me a few times before seeing one of his family members.

Because the first connection with Matt was so intense, I didn't think that it would become that intense again. I was wrong. Brenda had come to see me to again connect with Matt, which we did with no problem.

This time the reading took a different direction. Matt went into more detail about what was happening with the up-coming court case against the murderer and about his father's thoughts of taking revenge.. He insisted on sending messages to his father—messages to forgive and move on. Matt said that the man who killed him would kill again, and the next time would be much different. He insisted that everyone should know he is okay and that they need to be okay with it, too.

Matt showed me signs of protest and certain things about the news stations and newspapers. He also gave me a feeling that the man who had taken his life had gotten away with it. During this session with Brenda, Matt also kept bringing up the cemetery and saying that it was not a place she needed to go, that she should not feel that she needs to go there because he is not *at* the cemetery but with her. Brenda explained that she goes to the cemetery every day since Matt has passed. She also explained that Matt's father was very angry about the situation, as he had a right to be. This worried Brenda and seemed to concern Matt, according to some of his messages.

Matt did not come through as if he has forgiven the man but more as if he has accepted his fate to be on the other side. This was an important message that Matt has brought on many occasions. He wants everyone here to move on from this and accept it the best they can.

I could see a difference in Brenda's energy after seeing her the second time. Slowly but surely, the healing process for Brenda had begun and hopefully is the same for the rest of her family. But this was not the last time I would see Brenda or the last time I would connect with Matthew.

Brenda shared the rest of the story on her third visit to see me. This time she was a little more disturbed and upset about her situation. The police had finally given her Matthew's blood-stained clothes and personal items that they had been holding for evidence. Brenda was especially torn apart because of the outcome of the court trial.

It so happened that the man who killed Matthew and shot his friend had a connection with local politicians. The accused man was up for murder because he shot two young men, killing one. The district attorney was all out to have this man put away for life. Then, suddenly the case was dismissed. How do you shoot someone in the back, kill him, and get away with it? When I heard the story along with the messages Matt was bringing through during our sessions, I actually felt some of the pain Brenda was feeling. I could understand now why Matt came through worried about his own father and any actions he may want to take into his own hands. Matt did communicate that eventually, karma will take its path and the man who committed this murder will get what he deserves.

Matthew's Work on the Other Side

Time passed and so have several more sessions with Brenda and her daughter. Then I learned a lesson from my friend Matthew. Matt and I never actually met in the physical world, but at this point I feel as if he is my friend. During this session, Matt came through with his fun-loving personality as always, but this time more like a teacher giving a lecture. He asked everyone to try to move on from this and assured everyone that the man would reap some bad karma. Matt actually gave me a sense that the man was going to shoot someone again in the future. I hope that this is not the case. Then Matt talked about the cemetery and said he was glad to see a little moving on with the healing process.

Here, Brenda told me that the previous day was the first day she did not go to the cemetery. Matt made sure he let his mother know that he was ok with her not going and that it was actually what he preferred. Then Matt ended the reading, telling his mom that he wanted to be around her as much as possible. However, he mentioned that there is work on the other side for him to do. Seeing his family still suffering was not allowing him to move on to do other things that he needs to do—things I never realized they did on the other side until this particular day.

Matt said to his mom,

"I'm at St. Christopher's Hospital."

St. Christopher's Hospital is a well-known children's hospital in Philadelphia. Matt went on to explain the work he needs to carry out on the other side. Matt's spirit is in a higher realm now, meaning that he has learned what he needed to learn on earth and will not need to return. Matt said he now has his wings and is what we call an "angel." I got chills when Matt went on to tell his mother what he now does on the other side.

"Mom, I help the children at the hospital in a way that no one else can. I show them the light and help them to cross over to the other side."

This message fascinated me like no other message had. I never really knew what souls do on the other side when they cross over, nor did I imagine that they could do such amazing things for other souls. No doubt there is much work in different arenas for all souls. After that message, Matt's mother told me that Matt had a way with children, and they attached to him. After hearing that, it all makes even more sense.

Letting Go

Many souls do not want to cross over after they pass, especially young children. They attach themselves to their loved ones and refuse to go to the light. Sometimes this is because they do not understand or maybe they are afraid of the bright light. Young children don't understand things like death, and at times they don't even realize they have passed away. They think it's a dream. Matt has a very special job on the other side helping these children to see the light and not to fear it so they can cross over to where they need to be.

Children are not the only ones who have difficulty crossing over. People who have been murdered or have had other tragic deaths may hold on to living people such as family and other loved ones. If someone close to you has passed from a tragic death, suicide, or murder, you need to pray for them. Light a candle, call on them, and pray for them to go into the Light. Let them know there is love and peace in the Light and that other loved ones are waiting for them there. Let them know it is okay to cross over, and give them the permission to move on.

I cannot say that we are all going to cross over to become angels. I'm not even sure if everyone on the other side becomes an angel. I like to hope so, but probably not. I believe that only souls who are on a higher level become that of an angelic energy. They have learned their human lessons and need not return to earth to learn more. Now they go on to learn more of a spiritual angelic lesson working as an angel on the other side.

CHAPTER 11

The Psychic in You

II

The Psychic in You

Is everyone psychic? Many would say yes.

To a certain extent we are all psychic if we choose to tune in to that energy. However, I believe that some people, like myself, are born with a gift. I believe everyone is born with a some kind of gift (or gifts)—whether it is a psychic gift, a gift of acting, performing, singing, bringing joy to others, painting houses, or something else. Whether or not you choose to use your gift is entirely up to you. God has granted a gift to each of us, and we need to discover it within ourselves and do what we can with it. Unfortunately, many people either do not discover their gift, or they choose not to put it to good use.

We can all tap into psychic energy and intuition positively and safely. To work with psychic energy, you need to learn several methods of relaxation, creative visualization, and meditation. I believe it is also important that you have a positive healthy lifestyle. I try to keep my life balanced with as little drama as possible. I eat healthy, exercise, take vitamins, and try to get at least eight hours of sleep every night—all things that help me stay balanced with the work I do as a medium.

If you have the desire to tune in to the psychic energy within yourself or to work with your spirit guide, I have outlined a few exercises to help you accomplish these goals. I believe strongly in meditation for the growth of spirituality within yourself. Meditation can help you in many ways throughout your life. It will help you to put your mind at ease, to relax, and to breathe. Meditation will allow you to become in tune with your inner self and the energies that surround you.

Breathing Preparation

The first thing to do is to learn to breathe and relax. This is the hardest step in proper meditation. Find a place where you can sit and relax without interruption. I like to turn off the phone and play some soft meditative background music. Sit with your back straight and your feet flat on the floor. Or, you may sit crossed-legged. I do not recommend lying down, because you may fall asleep.

When you have found a comfortable place and have yourself situated, begin to practice your breathing. First, empty your lungs fully and hold for one second before taking a deep breath. Take the deepest breath you can without discomfort. When you breathe in deeply, hold it once more for one second. Exhale fully and hold again for one second before taking another deep breath. Continue breathing deeply and holding for one second on both your inhale and exhale.

Once you've breathed this way for a little while, you will understand why I say you have to practice often, especially your breathing exercise. If you are a beginner at meditation, I suggest working on the breathing for about one week before moving to the next step. When you do start meditating, your breathing will go into another pattern on its own when you are in a more relaxed meditative state.

The next step in meditation is to use your breathing to help you relax. This is the relaxation part of meditation. If you are a hypertense or nervous person whose mind will not stop, it may take you a bit longer to achieve a state of relaxation. However, as long as you can relax or at least sleep at night, you should have no problem achieving this state. Go back now to a place where you can sit and relax, free of interruptions with no phone calls.

1   Sit in a comfortable position with your feet on the floor and hands resting on your lap. Begin your breathing exercise, emptying your lungs and holding your breath for a second before inhaling fully. Continue your breathing.

2   Find a spot straight ahead just above eye level and stare and focus on this spot. Continue to breathe and allow your eyes to relax, to a point where they begin to get weary and tired from staring at your spot. The spot will begin to go out of focus and you will continue to breathe. Eventually, your eyelids will become heavy, and it will be hard for you to keep your eyes open.

3   Close your eyes and continue breathing. Your eyes are completely relaxed. Now, begin to relax your entire body, starting at your feet. Feel your feet and ankles begin to relax, breathe into that area of your body. As you exhale, say to yourself "relax." Feel your feet, ankles, knees, and legs begin to sink into the ground.

4   Work yourself upward, breathing into each area of the body and relaxing more and more each time you exhale. Work up into the buttocks, lower back, and spine. Continue to relax your shoulders and feel the relaxation going down your arms and into your hands and fingers. You will begin to feel as if you're sinking in a cotton cloud of relaxation, working up into your neck and head.

5   At this point, count down slowly from 10 to 1. As you count, you will go deeper into your relaxation.

    o   Begin with 10 and breathe in, 9 exhale saying to yourself relax, 8...7...6, going deeper now, even more relaxed; 5, relaxed, 4...3...2...1 and completely relaxed.

6   You may sit and enjoy this relaxed state for a bit before coming up out of the meditation. It is not recommended that you just open your eyes because it will leave you feeling nonrefreshed and tired. Come out of your meditation by counting upward from 1 to 10.

7   Say to yourself "I'm going to come out of my meditation by counting upward."

    o   Begin your count saying 1...2...3, coming up now, 4, more aware, 5, more aware, 6...7...8...9 and 10.

8   Now awake feeling refreshed and new again. This is a very basic relaxation/meditation in order to get you started.

Visualization

The next step may be a little difficult in the beginning but easy to master. Creative visualization is a very important step in the meditation process. It is the ability to visualize things with your mind and not your eyes. The easiest way to explain this is that it's very much like daydreaming, but with your eyes closed. While in a deep meditation, you should be able to create visual images and pictures of places with your mind's eye. You can use a simple exercise frequently to help you develop this skill.

1   Sit and relax with a lit candle about three feet in front of you at eye level.

2   Stare at the candle and into the candle flame for several minutes until your eyes begin to lose focus.

3   Close your eyes and relax them, keeping them still. Within sec-

onds, you should begin to see the candle's flame, and with a little focus you will even see the candle, its color, and its surroundings.

4   After practicing for at least 20 to 30 minutes with the candle lit, try the exercise again but put the candle out.

When you master this exercise, you can go on to other objects, and eventually you will be able to create your own images with your eyes closed.

Meditation

Now you have a good idea of basic relaxation and visualization, so that you can move on to the third exercise. This is what I like to call "The Peace Meditation." You begin with the relaxation exercise (above) to get yourself into a deep relaxation state. When you are completely relaxed, I will invite you to take yourself to a peaceful place, a place that you will create in your mind. This could be any place that you create where you feel at peace with the surroundings. It could be the beach, the park, beside a stream or waterfall, and any lovely place of your choosing.

5   Count slowly from 3 to I. When you reach I, you will be standing in your peaceful place. Three, beginning to relax even more, 2, and I.

6   Standing in your peaceful place, begin to look around at your surroundings. Just breathe and take in all the beauty that surrounds you. Listen to the sounds that are within your peaceful place, the sounds of nature. If your place is on the beach, listen to the ocean and the seagulls and feel the sand between your toes. Maybe your place is in the woods and you hear the sound of a stream with a small waterfall and in the distance a woodpecker peck, peck, pecking at a big oak tree.

7   Walk around a little until you find a nice place to sit within your peaceful surroundings—maybe up against a tree or on a rock that is carved out to fit your body. When you have found a place to sit, observe your surroundings. Begin to relax in your peaceful place.

8   At this point, you may choose to count yourself up out of the meditation, or you may go on into a deeper state—a state in which you will go deep into your subconscious and in which you will be able to connect with your spirit guides.

9   Now that you are relaxing in your peaceful place, begin to count down from 10 to 1, just as in your basic meditation. When you begin your count, tell yourself "with each number I will go deeper and deeper into a subconscious level; when I get to the number 1, I will be in a deep state of meditation."

Your mind should be completely at ease and you are feeling no stress whatsoever. At this level of consciousness, you are able to communicate with your spirit guides or guardian angels. We all have spirit guides; some have more than others. They are with you to guide you on a spiritual path. Your guides are not people you know who have passed. All your guides have been with you from the time you were brought into this world. They are angels of a higher existence than our souls are. They were appointed to you before you came to earth. They are just as anxious to communicate with you as you are with them.

1   While in your deep state of consciousness you may call on your guides for help in many aspects of life.

2   While sitting in your specially chosen spot in your special place, invite your guides to come.

3   Open your eyes in your special place and begin to look around and observe the scenery.

4   Off in the distance, you see a door that you create in your mind. This is the doorway for your guides to enter your special place. Invite them into your special place so that you may communicate with them and get to know them more. Don't be discouraged if they do not show themselves, this is not uncommon. So make sure you listen for them and pay attention to your surroundings. They sometimes appear in the form of another living creature such as a deer or a butterfly. If they do not appear or you are not hearing them, this is okay. It does not mean they are not there or that they do not exist. Practice makes perfect.

Alpha Meditation

Another meditation I like to use is what I call the alpha meditation. This allows me to open my seven chakras and put my mind into an alpha state. The alpha state is the state of consciousness that your mind drifts into right before sleep. Most of us, however, seem to skip the alpha state or move through it rather quickly before falling asleep. This is because of exhaustion from our hectic lives. When bedtime finally arrives, we drift off quickly into a deep sleep.

When I enter an alpha state and open my chakras, it allows me to better attune myself before I conduct my work as a medium. In the alpha state, our brain produces alpha waves. It is a powerful state of consciousness in which we can do things such as psychic work and healing. The chakras are energy points within the body where energy flows. (There are books on these energy centers in which you can read more about the chakras—how they work and how you can use the for healing.)

It is important to use the colors of the chakras in sequence to help yourself get into the alpha state of consciousness. To experience this meditation, you need to know the color, location, and number that correlates to each of the seven chakras.

1. The *first chakra* is located in the groin area at the base of the spine. Its color is red and its number is 7.

2. The *second chakra* is located just below the navel area. Its color is orange and its number is 6.

3. The *third chakra* is called the solar plexus and is located right below the center of the rib cage. Its color is yellow and it number is 5.

4. The *fourth chakra* is the heart chakra, obviously in the area of the heart. Its color is green and its number is 4.

5. The *fifth chakra* is the throat chakra located around the thyroid gland. Its color is blue and its number is 3.

6. The *sixth chakra* is important for all work with psychic energy. It is better known as the third eye chakra located between the eyebrows surrounding the pituitary gland. Its color is deep indigo and its number is 2.

7. The *seventh and last chakra* is the crown chakra, located at the top of the head surrounding the pineal gland. Its color is purple and its number is 1.

When you know where your chakras are located, make sure you understand their colors and numbers before beginning the following meditation. Once you have a full understanding, you may begin by finding a quiet place to sit and relax with your feet on the ground, hands on your lap, and your back is as straight as you can keep it with comfort.

Alpha Meditation Process

1. Begin by closing your eyes and taking a deep breath.
2. Release any emotions or frustrations from your hectic day.
3. Exhale all the air from your lungs and pause a moment before taking a deep full breath. Hold that breath a moment before exhaling.
4. With each exhale, make a loud vibrating sigh of relief.
5. Continue with your breathing and begin relaxing each part of your body starting with your feet and slowly working up to the top of your head. Don't rush into it, take your time and slowly relax.
6. Count from 10 to 1, relaxing yourself more and more with each number. When you get to 1, you will be completely relaxed.
7. Next, begin to visualize with your eyes closed a screen or maybe a TV in front of you. Now focus on your root chakra (first chakra).
8. On the screen, you will begin to see the color red form into the number 7.
9. Breathe in the color red and visualize a ball of red light spinning slowly in the area of your root chakra. You may even feel a tingling sensation in that area.
10. Next, move on to the navel chakra and visualize the color becoming orange. On the screen in front of you is the color orange forming the number 6.
11. Continue slowly working your way upward to the solar plexus and the yellow number 5. Then to the heart with its green number 4. Keep going until you reach the last chakra and its color.
12. At this point, say to yourself, "I'm now in an alpha state of consciousness." You may notice that your eyelids begin to flutter rapidly at times. This is a sure sign that you have achieved the alpha state of consciousness.

Enjoy this state of mind and use it to direct energy for healing others or use it for psychic work.

I always put myself into an alpha state before I do readings. I count myself down into alpha and then open my eyes to conduct my work as a psychic medium. When I'm finished my work, I close my eyes, relax, and count myself up out of the alpha state. You can do this by simply counting yourself back up from 1 to 7 out of the alpha state. Then you count yourself up from 1 to 10 to come out of your meditation.

Going Deeper

To achieve an even deeper state of mind, you may try the following exercise. I use this exercise before I read or do any type of past life work.

1   Once you have achieved the alpha state, begin to visualize a long hallway. At the end of the hallway, you find a stairway going down with 10 steps in all. Count yourself down the steps beginning with the number 10 and working down to the floor level number 1. Allow yourself to know that with each step you are going deeper and deeper into your subconscious mind.

2   When you reach the bottom of your staircase, you will see another hallway, this time with several doors. Each door is labeled to your preference. One door may say "past life" and another may say "spirit guides." Go on and explore your subconscious mind. Know that everything you do in this meditation is completely accurate and correct. Walk through the hallway while observing the doors, choose one door, and open it up and explore what is on the other side.

By now you should have a good idea of how to get yourself into a relaxed state and how to meditate. Relaxation and meditation will also help you become more in tune with the spiritual side of life and will help you become more in tune with your surroundings so that the next time your loved ones want to show you a sign of their presence, you will be ready.

□ □ □ □ □ □ □ □

I hope by now that you have learned that your loved ones are doing well on the other side. There is no pain or discomfort for those who have crossed. We do not take our illnesses or any other negative emotions with us when we cross over. Know that your loved ones are not mad or disappointed in you in any way. Most important, know that they visit us on special occasions like birthdays and anniversaries, and especially when we are having a difficult time.

Remember that we are all here to learn many lessons and we cannot expect those who have passed on to help us with these lessons. They can be with us in spirit giving comfort to our souls, but they cannot interfere with or help us with a lesson we came here to learn. Know that your loved ones are with you and are aware of the things going on in your life. They have seen you growing up and have seen your children born. And one day you will see them again.

For further information on Joseph Tittel, his newsletter, seminars, and meditation CD's, you may write to him at:

Joseph Tittel
PO Box 1299
Levittown, PA 19058-1299

Or please visit one of his web sites at:

http://www.spiritmanjoseph.com

http://www.messagesfromtheotherside.com